FIVE EASY STEPS TO ACHIEVING YOUR GOALS
NOW!

HOW TO BUILD YOUR TOOL BOX FOR A GOAL SETTING PLAN DESIGNED FOR ACHIEVEMENT.

By

Kenneth R. Grow

Published by Old Oak Media Partners, LLC

Five Easy Steps to Achieving Your Goals Now!

How to build your tool box for a goal setting plan designed for achievement.

Kenneth R. Grow

Copyright © 2013 Old Oak Media Partners, LLC
Downey, California

Printed in the U.S.A.

All rights reserved; no part of this publication may be reproduced, stored in a retrieval system, or transmitted in any form or by any means, electronic, mechanical, photocopying, recording, or otherwise, without the prior written permission of Old Oak Media Partners, LLC.

Library of Congress Catalog Card Number: 2012950285

ISBN 13: 978-0615702889

ISBN 10: 0615702880

Success, Personal Growth, Self-Help, Self-Improvement

Dedication

*To my wife Carol and our children,
for all they have taught me.*

Table of Contents

Dedication iii

About the Author xi

Acknowledgments xiii

Introduction xv

Step One: Keep It Simple

  Chapter 1 1

    Keep It Simple 2

    Bite-Size It 4

    Show No Fear 5

    Where Are You Right Now? 7

    What's Your Take? 10

    Get Your Notebook 11

Step Two: Keep It Real

  Chapter 2 15

    Keep It Real 15

    How Real Is It? 18

    Time and Reality 21

    Hold Your Feet to the Fire 24

    What's Your Take? 24

    Get Your Notebook 26

Step Three: Focus on the Achievable

  Chapter 3 29

    Focus on the Achievable 29

    How Achievable Is It? 30

    Time Frames 32

    Organizing 34

    What's Your Take? 37

    Get Your Notebook 38

Step Four: Define Your Plan

  Chapter 4 41

    Define Your Plan 41

    Set Your Stepping-Stones 43

    Achievable and Timely 44

    Prioritize 48

    What's Your Take? 50

    Get Your Notebook 51

  Chapter 5 55

    Keep Your Balance 55

    Weighting Each Facet 57

    Sacrifice 58

    Due Diligence 60

    What's Your Take? 63

    Get Your Notebook 65

  Chapter 6 69

    Facets of Our Life – Health and Family 69

    Health Facet 70

    Diet 72

    Exercise 72

    Family Facet 75

    Relationships 76

    What's Your Take? 78

    Get Your Notebook 79

Chapter 7 83
    Facets of Our Life – Spirituality, Self-Improvement,
    and Community 83
    Spirituality Facet 84
    Self-Improvement/Education Facet 86
    Community Facet 89
    What's Your Take? 91
    Get Your Notebook 92

Chapter 8 97
    Facets of Our Life – Career and Finances 97
    Career Facet 98
    Finances Facet 101
    What's Your Take? 104
    Get Your Notebook 106

Step Five: Take Action

Chapter 9 111
    Take Action 111
    Take Action Now 112
    What's Your Take? 122
    Get Your Notebook 123

Chapter 10 127
    Measuring Your Progress 127
    Defining Progress 128
    Measuring Progress 129
    Defeating Fear 132
    What's Your Take? 134
    Get Your Notebook 135

Chapter 11	139
The New Paradigms	139
Health	140
Family	141
Spirituality	142
Self-Improvement/Education	143
Community	144
Career	145
Finances	146
What's Your Take?	147
Get Your Notebook	149
Chapter 12	153
Grab Your Tools and Get To Work	153
Opportunity	154
Responsibility	155
Ownership	155
Limitations	156
The Future	157
Your Tool Box	158

Appendixes

Personal Inventory Summary	163
Health Facet	164
Family Facet	167
Spirituality Facet	169
Self-Improvement/Education Facet	172
Community Facet	177
Career Facet	179

Finances Facet 181
Additional Areas You Wish To Set Goals In 184
Simple Budget 185
Goal Setting Form 187
Action Step Form 189

About the Author

KENNETH R. GROW has a master's degree in business administration. He has written books and conducted workshops about setting goals since 1977.

He has worked in large corporations and small businesses, and has owned several businesses.

He has worked in vocational development and job skills training, teaching individuals how they can achieve their goals if they have a plan to follow.

After years of success helping those in the workplace, he decided to share his knowledge and experiences in this book.

Ken and his wife, Carol, live in Downey, California, where they raised their family.

Acknowledgments

THIS BOOK WOULD NOT have been possible without the help and encouragement of my family, friends, and the many mentors who taught me by example.

I am indeed grateful for all those who shared their wisdom and insight from their life's experiences. I learned that I was not alone in looking toward the future. The future was up to me to plan if I wanted to realize my dreams.

There are not enough words to truly express how appreciative I am to my parents and my wife's parents for setting me on this journey. They seemed to always find time for a teaching moment when I needed one. It was always done with love, encouragement and for me to seek improvement and knowledge, followed by a reminder to share that knowledge with others.

Introduction

THIS BOOK WAS WRITTEN to help those who have never set a goal, and for those who have set goals and had varying levels of success in achieving them. Each of us is unique, but there are many things we have in common. We have a desire to be more successful in the things that matter to us most. Some will place a great deal of emphasis on their families. Others might place their emphasis on their careers.

Our family, for the most part, is what motivates us to work, to improve our talents, skills, and abilities. The more knowledge we obtain, the better we can share with our family, friends, and co-workers. In addition, we are always hoping for an increase in our wages. The best way to get a raise is to increase our value to our employer. This is achieved by increasing our knowledge, skills, and abilities.

The best way to increase your worth is to set a goal to find out what is required to move to the next level. You can accomplish this by listing the requirements and then doing an honest personal inventory to see if you meet some of those requirements. You may find that you have only a few to address, or you may find that you are far short of meeting those requirements. Once you know where you stand, you can create a plan to gain the knowledge, skills, and abilities needed. Next, you have to take action. Without taking action you will never accomplish your goals.

Goal setting is somewhat personal, yet if you ask your family, friends, or supervisor, you will see that you have plenty of support. Most of us like to see individuals overcome obstacles and achieve success. We all need to improve something in our lives, no matter who we are or where we are in life.

Offering to help someone achieve his or her goals by being a mentor, or encouraging that person to move forward, is a gift to the individual and a gift to the one offering the help. We can do many things on our own, but often we owe gratitude to someone else who helped in our accomplishment. Even if the help came from a book written many years ago, that author helped make it possible to achieve your goal.

Don't be afraid that you might fail. Failure is when you give up and refuse to try again. Not all the goals you write down will be achieved. You will find that some goals you wrote down were not really goals. If you make your goals simple, real, achievable, defined, and then to take action, you will be surprised how easy it is to achieve them. But first, you will have to overcome your fear of change. Face fear with a solid plan and you will overcome the obstacles you might encounter. Go forward bravely and accomplish your dreams. You can do it. You will do it. Use the tools you will gain in this book.

Kenneth R. Grow

STEP ONE

Keep It Simple

CHAPTER 1

Keep It Simple

*Whatever the mind of man can
conceive and believe it can achieve.*
Napoleon Hill

WE ALL HAVE DREAMS, we all have desires. We want to achieve success and reach our goals. You have probably run into the same wall many others have in trying to set and accomplish your goals: *"How do I do it?" "Where do I start?"*

You begin by keeping it simple. You break your goals into bite-sized, manageable steps that lead directly to reaching your goals. Be brave and show no fear. The changes you make will be those you select. Know where you want to go and where you are starting from.

An English Franciscan friar named William of Ockham, who lived in Ockham, Surrey, England during the fourteenth century, is credited with the principle *"Entities should not be multiplied unnecessarily."* That is, one must shave off all nonessentials, leaving only the simplest solution. This principle is known as **Occam's Razor** and can be distilled to the following quote:

"Keep it simple."

FIVE EASY STEPS TO ACHIEVING YOUR GOALS NOW!

Keep It Simple

The best way to tackle your goals is to make them simple. I don't mean choosing only those easy, "low-hanging fruit," "anyone can do it" goals that offer a sense of false achievement. You can have bold and grand goals that are simple, not just simplistic. Simple defined here means uncomplicated, yet not necessarily easy.

We often try to apply too much misplaced logic or thought into making things more complicated than we should. Sometimes when the simplest solution is available, we tend to think it can't be that simple. We often think complicated is more effective than simple. It is just in our nature to do so.

The first thing you have to accept is that you should do no more than you can do. Certainly I am not advocating that you drop everything else in your life and only eat, drink, and breathe your goals. Time is a constraint that binds us, but we can control how we spend it. It is ours to use productively or wastefully. However, remember, that once it is over, each moment of time is gone. There is no way to create time. It is gone forever.

There is nothing too difficult here, unless you choose to make it so. Each step you take should move you closer to your goal. If you are not moving toward your goal, you are moving away from it. Many others have achieved goals similar to yours. The secret they found is keeping it simple, not making it more difficult or complicated.

Each chapter will have a box entitled **CASE NOTE** written from real life experiences to provide a better understanding of the subject matter being presented.

KEEP IT SIMPLE

CASE NOTE

Over the years I have successfully completed three fifty mile hikes in the High Sierra Mountains of central California. When asked, "How did you do it?" I just say, "One step at a time."

It was a bit more involved than that. I first had to complete several training hikes. Then there were several more conditioning hikes. And there was a shake-down hike to make sure all the necessary gear and equipment were packed, tested, and good to go.

These pre-hikes prepared me and the rest of my group for the ultimate goal: a week of hiking fifty miles in the mountains. Each hike had a theme or purpose to prepare us for what food we would take and what type of clothing would be required. Each member of the group was given additional training in first aid. Physical exams were required to make sure all were healthy enough to make the journey.

Permits were required, and we had to apply for the dates we wanted to be on the trail and reserve the campsites we intended to stay at. Transportation was also critical. The logistics at first seemed to overwhelm the novices, but with the help of some seasoned hikers, we were able to break things down into bite-sized pieces. Each bite-sized piece made the whole goal of enjoying the beauty of the High Sierras a reality. **One step at a time!**

FIVE EASY STEPS TO ACHIEVING YOUR GOALS NOW!

Bite-Size It

When you see a delicious-looking apple pie, you never try to put the entire pie into your mouth. You make the task easier by eating it in bite-sized pieces. Reducing things to a proper and manageable size makes them easier to accomplish.

When you make your goals simple, it is easier to see what steps will be required to reach them. You take one step at a time. There will be a logical order in which to put the bite-sized steps that will lead to successfully achieving each of your goals. In turn each goal you reach puts you that much closer to your ultimate goal.

Creating bite-sized steps leading to your goal is no different from creating simple goals. Taking on more than you can do will only delay and discourage you, and possibly cause you to abandon your goal. Following the rule to keep it simple is one of the best things you can do for yourself.

By placing your bite-sized portions in order, you will create a time line allowing you to quantify, qualify, and visually realize what you will need to do. You will see your growth and accomplishments better. Keeping them in a proper order of completion will make sure you do not accidentally skip something that will later be an obstacle that might derail your efforts.

Please read aloud the pledge in the following box. Repeat it two more times. Read it and *mean* it again in the morning when you get up and before retiring at night. Burn this pledge into your mind and subconscious so it will be a habit you employ in each goal you set.

Write it on a three-by-five card and place it on the bathroom mirror where you will see it often. Each time you see it, repeat it aloud. Repeat it again until you say it with bold confidence and you truly believe it. This will help you understand the meaning of making things simple. Simple allows you to achieve your goals without distractions, permanent obstructions, or confusion. Simple makes focusing on the important things clearer, sharper, and more achievable.

> **MY PLEDGE**
> *I will make all things simple.*
> *I will only do that which I can do effectively.*
> *I will enjoy this journey into a new paradigm.*

Show No Fear

Our lives are full of various paradigms. These are the situations, conditions, and circumstances we are currently holding on to. The circumstances and conditions you live in, combined with your education and life experiences, are what define you as an individual. You are unique. Yet there are many things that we all share in common.

Do not fear the unknown, for everything can be learned. This will help reduce the uncertainty and stress haunting you. At the beginning of this endeavor, you may have some doubts about your ability to make the needed changes in your life. You need to make changes to move toward your new paradigm. One reason you are reading this book is to move yourself from where you are now to where you want to be. So do you now find yourself in a situation, condition, or circumstance you would like to change?

Many of us are afraid to make changes. We fear the unknown. When we have a strong desire to change, we have to face our individual situation and decide where we want to be. When we do change from our current situation to another, what takes place is referred to as a paradigm shift.

Remember, others have done what you are about to do. They have survived and have gone on to tell how they managed it. This actually makes it easier since many of the steps and suggestions in this book have been proven when tested by both time and circumstance. We are each unique as individuals, yet we all have desires to achieve more than what we have now. You hope to live a better life, being more knowledgeable and more charitable. Helping others will provide a tremendous amount of personal satisfaction when you reach that point in your life.

> *"If you think you can, you can. If you think you can't, you're right!"*
>
> *Mary Kay Ash*

Deal only with the things that you can control. Don't let outside influences cause you to abandon your dreams and goals. Life will challenge you often, but you will develop the ability to recognize what you can control and how to control it. You will have some imperfections. We all have some. They can be overcome with increased knowledge, skills, talents, and abilities. If you lack knowledge, go to the library or ask someone who you feel will be willing to help you do some research. If you don't ask for help, you may never get it. By seeking support, you increase the odds a thousand percent in your favor of getting what you need to achieve your goals.

There are things out of your control, such as the weather, the tide, and the seasons. You can, however, control your attitude. And that alone makes you very powerful. Your attitude and how you see things will help you deal with the outside influences that will test your strength. Some things might require you to make a change or reevaluate an action step. Don't let little things cause you to lose sight of your ultimate goal. Consider this journey as leading to a new you, a learning experience opening up new opportunities and insight into who you truly are, or can be.

Where Are You Right Now?

This is the first question that must be answered before you can begin to make this transformation. Yes, you will be transformed into whatever your goals are. This is why you must first define where you are now. You have to identify your current personal paradigm. This consists of where and what you are right now and the individual circumstances that bind you.

What is your highest level of education? What skills do you have? What special abilities do you possess? What do you know at this moment about what you expect after you achieve your goal? Go ahead and list some of your general

FIVE EASY STEPS TO ACHIEVING YOUR GOALS NOW!

goals. Then go back and list what effect they will have and how your life will be changed. Be honest, and in some cases, be hard on yourself. If you can survive your own critique, it will help you take the criticism others might direct at you.

Next begin to prioritize your goals. What is the most important goal at this moment? What is the least important? What couple of goals would be nice to accomplish? Answer these objectively and you will be closer to reaching your goals.

To get anywhere, you need an accurate beginning and ending point. Identifying your correct starting point and knowing where you want to be makes getting there possible and much easier. It will save time and wasted effort that can be used more effectively in working toward your goals.

In the appendixes of this book and in the available companion workbook, you will find a personal inventory summary. Take time to study it and complete it honestly. You will see many of your goals are almost within reach. A personal assessment or inventory is always a great place to start. It is written by you. Who knows you better than you? No one! You don't have to share it with anyone if you don't want to. It is yours and only yours. It is just another tool to help you move faster toward achieving your goals.

"You are free to choose, but the choices you make today will determine what you will have, be, and do in the tomorrow of your life!"

Zig Ziglar

In the following chapters, you will be introduced to

other tools to help you on this journey. Keeping records of your successes and accomplishments will help you see that you are indeed making progress. Sometimes it will seem slow and even burdensome when progress appears to be eluding you. Don't despair. You can make adjustments to see if you might have better results. Try another angle. Look at things from a different perspective. You might find that something else works even better than what you first had planned.

Above all else stay the course. Keep focusing and working daily on your action steps, and they will take you to your goals. Find the time, make the time to do what you have to do. Don't look for excuses — they are not acceptable. You should expect the best from yourself. You can do it.

Remember to keep it simple. Don't overdo it by trying to accomplish too much and becoming discouraged. Break things down into bite-sized action steps you can accomplish quickly. Your cumulative accomplishments are what will eventually get you to your goals. Take each step and enjoy the journey toward your goals.

Do things in order so you stay on course. Remember, this is an evolutionary time line which must be followed in order to reach success. Celebrate your growth and enjoy the journey. Gather the knowledge and skills you now lack. Don't let outside influences cause you to doubt your chances for success. You can succeed. You will succeed!

Don't forget to be honest and do the personal inventory summary. You must have the correct starting point, which is where you are at this moment. This makes it faster to plot the course to your goals, which increases the chances of achieving your goals.

In chapter 2 you will be introduced to how to keep your goals realistic. An action step or goal that is not realistic is a waste of time and resources. You now know how to keep your goals simple.

Do yourself proud! Make success part of your daily routine.

What's Your Take?

At the end of each chapter, you will be asked to complete an assignment. You might think of it as a test, quick quiz, or a personal reflection. It will help you see if you understand the material you have read. These questions are for you to answer honestly and sincerely. This will only be seen by you or anyone you have helping you achieve your goals. You will have the opportunity to answer additional questions at the end of this book so you can compare your thoughts at this stage and see how differently you feel at the conclusion of the book.

It is recommended that you have a notebook or binder in which you can record your answers. Write down the assignment and write down your answers and thoughts. Identify which chapter you are writing about and date it.

Hold yourself to a higher standard and you will see a more successful you.

Get Your Notebook

1. Write down exactly what you expect to achieve from this book.

2. Write what you can do to prepare yourself to move forward in your life.

3. List any obstacles you know of right now that might interfere with your being willing, able, or ready to move forward at this time.

4. From the list you made above, pick one obstacle and write how you can overcome it.

5. Write down the most important concept you learned from this chapter and how it impressed you.

STEP TWO

Keep It Real

CHAPTER 2

Keep It Real

*If there is a sense of reality,
there must also be a sense of possibility.*
Robert Musil

WE HAVE ALL DREAMED of just sitting on the beach under a nice umbrella sipping on our favorite drink without any care or worry in the world. We know reality will soon snap us out of this dream. And then we begin to think of all the things we still have to do to get through the day, let alone the rest of our lives.

You must write your action steps and goals with reality in mind. Put your action steps and goals to a reality test. Make sure they will move you toward your goal. If you need to obtain some education or skill, then make it a priority goal with appropriate action steps. You will also have to consider if the action step or goal can be accomplished in a realistic amount of time. Remember, these are your goals and you have to hold yourself accountable.

Keep It Real

You know at the end of the day it is the real things that matter. Reality is what you live in. Still, we all want to escape to paradise once in a while, away from the stress, noise, and turmoil of the daily grind.

FIVE EASY STEPS TO ACHIEVING YOUR GOALS NOW!

Imagination is the spring of innovation and invention. If you can imagine what it would be like to be in a different paradigm, then there is hope it can become a real possibility. But I must caution you that too wild or improbable imaginings can be very dangerous to pursue. The side bar on this page is just one illustration to consider.

> When we are small children, our imaginations tend to get ahead of the realities of life. Perhaps we just need to mature to be able to see that what we can do and what we would like to do are not always the same.
>
> Young boys, speaking from experience, think they can fly if they run and jump off the roof of the house. Immediately the law of gravity is in effect. A higher source is telling us we are not capable of flying on our own.
>
> **"Keep it real."**

You are capable of flying as a passenger in some sort of aircraft. That piece of machinery was designed to lift off the ground and take flight. Good thing they also figured out how to safely land it!

You have to be honest and accept the limitations you have. They are real and may restrict your ability to achieve some goals.

If you are lacking education, this is a reality you must face. I know that going back to school after many years in the work force is very hard to do. If this is what you need to do, accept reality and plan some shorter-term goals to deal with this obstacle. Don't wallow in self-pity and say it is too hard. I have worked for years with many individuals who have taken control of their lives, and if education was an issue, they addressed it. They made this a priority and did it. They are the individuals who see what is really needed and are not afraid to go after it.

Keep your goals real. Keep them in the proper perspective. You should be in control of your goals, not have your goals controlling you. Some of the goals you choose to pursue might temporarily overlap or conflict with some of your other goals. This is the time to be real and make a choice. Decide which goal needs to be completed first and finish it.

Real action steps and goals can be achieved. Unrealistic action steps and goals are a waste of time to even plan. They can drain you of productive progress and sidetrack you from where you really want to be. Check to see if your goals are really going to get you there. Don't assume that because you have them in writing, they are real. Real means you can achieve them. Real means they will be stepping-stones to the next level. Real means you will see progress and personal growth.

Be careful and don't over-commit yourself. You will have several goals that are great and will eventually get you where you want to go. Be prepared to run into obstructions, set-backs, and self-doubts. This is normal. Some of these will be very real. Others will only seem real if you give them any credence.

Remember, this is an evolutionary journey. It will take some time to reach your goal. Keep your plan simple and real. It is fine to have some dreams. Certainly I am not trying to squash your dreams. I just want to see you have goals with some sense of reality and possibility of being achieved.

> **CASE NOTE**
>
> Over the years, many whom I have worked with would set a goal they were not ready for. Some would want to be a doctor or some other professional as their career goal. They did not have a high school diploma. Though they felt they could do it, reality would always prevail. If you will need an education, then get it first. It is never too late to start. However, the longer you take to get started, the longer it will take to reach your goals.

How Real Is It?

Here are some simple steps you can take to make sure your goals are real. First, do you know people who have been in your situation and who have changed their lives in the direction you would like yours to go? If so, ask them what steps they took to get there. Ask them if they found it easy or hard. Did they have some second thoughts about what course of action they took?

These questions are the easiest of the tests to see if your goal is real. Finding people who have been through this before and who have accomplished similar goals lets you know that it must be real. If you are able to find someone to mentor you, he or she may be able to help you assess how real your goal is. Your mentor should be someone with a bit more experience and knowledge than you about where you want to be.

I know and have known many individuals who are far more successful and knowledgeable than I am. They treated me and my questions with due respect and were willing to take the time to make sure I fully understood what they were teaching me. Sometimes I was not as smart as I should have been and did not put their suggestions into practice when I should have. But from experience I have learned much, sometimes well after I should have seen the light!

> *"Remember that not getting what you want is sometimes a wonderful stroke of luck."*
>
> *The Dalai Lama*

A very impressive American dream was to have a man land on the moon. Many things had to be in place to make this possible. Think of the thousands of years it took to develop the mathematics, metallurgy, scientific advancements, communication technologies, and training procedures—training not only for the astronauts, but also all the support teams, vendors, and suppliers. Each space mission or rocket launch preceding the lunar landing had a purpose. Each purpose was a stepping-stone leading to the ultimate goal of getting man on the moon.

Each action step you take should be looked at as a stepping-stone leading to reaching your goal. If you do not have a realistic action step, you will not make progress toward your goal. You must accept and deal with your current limitations when planning a real goal.

If you need to learn a skill or craft before you can proceed toward your goal, you must first acquire that skill or craft. It could be a financial requirement that is holding you back. Plan a realistic goal that will allow you to earn the money you will need. Don't overextend yourself, and stay within your limits. Staying out of debt is easy. Don't get into debt in the first place! I know that most of us have had some rough patches in our lives because of financial issues. If you need help, there are plenty of resources where you can get help for very little money or at no cost.

Can your action step or goal pass the smell test? (I really mean a possibility test.) I have had goals that were realistic, but at that stage in my life they were not practical or possible. There were obstacles that I had to overcome and skills, talents, and abilities that I had to acquire before I was ready to move forward. The longer you put it off, the longer it will be before you achieve your ultimate goal. Time is of the essence, and as the saying goes, *time and tide wait for no man.*

Also, you must realize that an unrealistic goal is not in your best interest, no matter how much you might like to achieve it. These types of goals may be too costly financially, emotionally, or physically for you to succeed. If you put honest and sincere thought into each of your goals you should see the path you will need to take. Just be sure you really want to go there before you start. Again, time and opportunity will be wasted if the goal is not realistic.

Please read aloud a new pledge in the following pledge box. By repeating it you will make it part of your thoughts. Read this pledge until it becomes an automatic habit. You will employ this pledge in each goal you set. Write it on a three-by-five card and place it on the bathroom mirror where you will see it often. Each time you see it, repeat it aloud. Repeat it again until your mind makes it part of your daily routine. This will help you understand the meaning of keeping your goals real. Real so you can achieve your goals without distractions, permanent obstructions, or confusion. Real makes focusing on the important things clearer, sharper, and more achievable.

> **MY PLEDGE**
> *I will make all goals real.*
> *I will do a reality check on each goal.*
> *I will enjoy this journey into a new paradigm.*

Time and Reality

Time and reality can work together, or they can work individually against you. If you plan a realistic goal, it must include the time in which you must accomplish it in order to stay on target for your ultimate goal. We all are guilty of procrastination. *"I will do it tomorrow or next week."* Sound familiar?

FIVE EASY STEPS TO ACHIEVING YOUR GOALS NOW!

Remember, you read in the previous chapter that time is fleeting and cannot be increased or regained. If you think you cannot afford to work on your goals due to financial limitations, time is by far the more valuable commodity that you have available to accomplish your goals.

You will have to invest your time and other resources in order to change your life. If you are going to make any investment, you need to know the potential profit before you make that commitment by making a risk assessment. Most of us will only invest in that which is realistic. Sure, we all have made some dumb investments and lost both time and money. We could have made money if we had only ascertained there was a real possibility that the venture would be worth it.

Just how much time you will use or invest in accomplishing your goal is determined by the time frame of the goal itself. Goals are usually broken down into several time frame categories. These categories are important to understand because if you place a goal into the wrong category, you may delay achievement or try to accomplish a goal before you are ready.

The big or ultimate goals you can label as your life goals. These usually have a time frame of ten years or longer to achieve. You will have other goals that will be taking you toward your life goal, and each must be kept in perspective and in a logical order.

Long-term goals are anything that you should be able to complete or achieve within the next ten years. These goals should be taking you toward your ultimate goal. Medium-term goals are those that you should be able to handle within a two-year window. Short-term goals are those that can be completed within six months. The simple action steps are things you should be able to complete within one to two weeks. Consider these terms and the action steps and goals as the foundation you are building to support your ultimate life goal or goals.

Action steps can and should be easy to accomplish. Keeping them simple and within their time frame will help you realize meaningful and measurable success. Many action steps will be employed to achieve the short-term goals you establish for yourself. Many of the short-term goals will help you achieve your medium-term, long-term and life goals.

> *"What we achieve inwardly will change outer reality."*
>
> *Plutarch*

You can set up any tracking system you feel comfortable with, one that you are willing and able to follow. One of the first things you need to do is to create a time line showing your goals leading to your life goals. Between then and now, place what long-term, medium-term and short-term goals you must achieve. Then fill in what action steps you need to accomplish within the next couple of weeks. Each step moves you closer to your ultimate goal.

A daily calendar notebook is fine since you can list your goals at the point of when you want to complete them and then work back to where you are now. Some individuals have success with writing down their goals on colored three-by-five index cards, each color representing a time frame. A different colored card is used for the action steps that will be required. This system is flexible—you can rearrange the cards, insert new cards, or remove cards for action steps that are no longer needed.

You can use any system you are comfortable with. Use a white board, a growth chart, or a poster board. Whatever system you choose to use, be sure to have space to write down resources and individuals that can help you with each step. Be sure to list any training, skill set, or knowledge that will help you achieve success.

Hold Your Feet to the Fire!

Self-discipline is a must since these are your goals, your desires, and your aspirations. This is all yours. You are responsible for accomplishing your goals. Be a firm taskmaster and push yourself. Once you are making progress, you will be able to see your dedication is paying off. Enlist the help of a mentor or someone who cares about you and wants to see you succeed. Let him or her cheer you on to success.

You have now learned how to keep your goals simple and real. In chapter 3 you will learn how to keep your goals achievable. You are off to a great start. Keep up the good work.

Do your best. Improve each day and soon success will arrive.

What's Your Take?

At the end of this chapter, you are asked to complete your assignment. You might think of it as a test, quick quiz, or a personal reflection. It will help you see if you understand the material you have read in this chapter. These questions are for you to answer honestly and sincerely.

Success is nearly yours. You will achieve your goals.

FIVE EASY STEPS TO ACHIEVING YOUR GOALS NOW!

Get Your Notebook

1. Write down your definition of what makes a realistic goal.

2. Write down a few realistic goals you are thinking of and how you will keep them real.

3. List any obstacles that you know of right now that might interfere with your being willing, able, or ready to move forward at this time.

4. From the list you made above, pick one and write how you can overcome the obstacle.

5. Write down the most important concept you learned from this chapter and how it impressed you.

STEP THREE

Focus on the Achievable

CHAPTER 3

Focus on the Achievable

Success is about enjoying what you have and where you are, while pursuing achievable goals.
Bo Bennett

YOU CERTAINLY MUST HAVE a sharp focus on what you want to achieve. However, you need to realize that not everything you want will be achievable. It may not be what is best for you. It may not be achievable due to circumstances you have no control over.

The American author Zane Grey once stated:

"I arise full of eagerness and energy, knowing well what achievement lies ahead of me."

Your goals will need to be set in their proper time frame. Don't be guilty of shortchanging yourself by not allowing enough time or taking too much time for each step. You will be required to stay organized in order to accomplish your goals. Reviewing your goal is as important as setting the goal. If it is worth working on, it is worth reviewing.

Focus on the Achievable

As you write down your goals, you must focus on

each one and decide whether you can or should achieve a particular goal at this time. Even a goal that is very realistic and is achievable may not be in your best interest. It might have an immediate negative impact on your life or your family, or be unwarranted at this particular time in your life.

Your goal should be in the direction you would like to go. If there are obstacles or detours in that direction, you may be delayed. You will have wasted time and energy that could have been better spent elsewhere.

The reason you need to put your action steps in order is so you won't possibly skip one. The one you skip could be a foundation for several other action steps. Things will go faster if you work on achievable goals at the proper stage and time. Remember to think achievable and not be lost in a fantasy world.

How Achievable Is It?

Use some quick tests to see if your goal is achievable. Will you actually accomplish something that is in the direction of your ultimate goal when completed? Many have worked hard on an action step or short-term goal that did not result in the original expectation. At times your efforts might take you a bit off course. No matter how far you go, you are not progressing if you are going in the wrong direction. You will have to start all over and make modifications or serious adjustments, which could have been avoided if you had tested for achievability.

Another easy test is to ask yourself if you have the resources you will require at this moment to successfully

FOCUS ON THE ACHIEVABLE

complete your action step or goal. These resources can include the skill, ability, knowledge, and willingness to move forward at this time.

> **CASE NOTE**
>
> I have worked with many who had a strong desire to move forward in their lives but lacked the willingness to make any attempt. They blame anything and everything for why they cannot move forward. They fail to recognize they are the obstacle or obstruction to their own progress.
>
> Some will boldly jump in and just go for it. It doesn't take long before they realize they are in way over their heads. Why? They never took the time to plan or set their goals to be achieved.

Seek help from a mentor or someone you trust. Perhaps you know someone who has done this before or been in the same situation. Remember, all is not lost. With a little bit of help you can easily be brought back on track. Make sure you are still heading in the direction you want to go.

"Optimism is the faith that leads to achievement. Nothing can be done without hope and confidence."

Helen Keller

Sometimes it is just about your own ego. You have to do it your way even if you have been told you should not. When working on goals, and especially testing to see if an action step or goal is achievable, you may let your heart lead you rather than your common sense. You should have a strong passion for your goals, but at the same time, make sure you can achieve them.

Do you know anyone who has achieved this goal? If not, you might have to do some more research, or at least direct some questions to someone who can help you. You might require a substantial financial investment to acquire the skills and knowledge to achieve the goal. This is going to be hard if you don't have the financial resources. An action step or short-term goal to earn some of the required funding might be considered a first step.

Time Frames

Many of your action steps will be easy and achievable. They will cost little or nothing to accomplish. Time, for the most part, will be your largest investment in achieving your goals. Action steps are to be accomplished in one to two weeks. We discussed the time frames in chapter 2.

Be honest and make sure your action steps and short-term goals are really moving you toward your desired goal. Each action step should be treated with the same passion as any of your long-term or life goals.

While you are on this journey, you may alter or change some of your medium-term, long-term or life goals. This does not mean you have to scrap everything and start anew. It will show a new direction. This may be better for you. The accomplishments made so far may still be valid for the newly-revised goal. Think of it as coming to a fork in a road.

FOCUS ON THE ACHIEVABLE

One road you will find going toward your original plan, and the other in the direction of something new that will prove to be more beneficial.

The ability to see and recognize opportunities is one of the greatest benefits of working toward any worthwhile goal. You may discover the original goal has lost some of its shine as you get closer. You may find a better and more profitable opportunity waiting for you elsewhere.

All things achievable will be bound by time. Proper selection of your time frame is essential. Most individuals will begin with the end in mind. This is good since you will have some idea of where you want to be. Then you just work from where you are now to fill in the required steps to get you there.

For example, your dream career will require that you have at least a bachelor's degree. You only have a high school diploma and a couple of college credits for an art class you thought you would enjoy. You know that a medium-term goal would be to obtain enough credits to meet the minimum requirement for the position you would like to be in. Your short-term goal will be to enroll in those courses and start earning the credits needed.

The first action step will be to find out just what classes you will have to take. Your next action step will be to enroll in the classes offered during next semester's enrollment. Once enrolled, your short-term goal will be to attend classes, study, and pass the required examinations. Weekly action steps will be the number of pages you will read or study in order to pass those tests.

Again, tracking your accomplishments and celebrating your achievements throughout this journey are required. You deserve to pat yourself on the back. But don't forget to set new action steps for the next phase you need to complete so you are always moving toward your goal.

Read aloud another new pledge in the following box. Put this pledge into your mind and subconscious so it will be an automatic habit you use in each goal you set. Place it on the bathroom mirror where you will see it often, along with the others you have written. Read them all aloud again until you say them with conviction. This will help you understand the meaning of making your goals achievable. Do things in order so you can achieve your goals without distractions, permanent obstructions, or confusion. By keeping goals achievable, you make focusing on the important things clearer, sharper, and more doable.

> **MY PLEDGE**
> *I will make all goals achievable.*
> *I will achieve success one step at a time.*
> *I will enjoy this journey into a new paradigm.*

Organizing

We will not be going into project management layout and design. However, if you understand how to manage a project, you will understand how effective a tool it can be.

FOCUS ON THE ACHIEVABLE

Making a time line is good for tracking your progress toward your goals.

This is important so you can see the time you need to complete each step in order to reach your goals. Organization is the key here. You should be able to spot congestions and dead spaces. Once you are actively engaged in this process, you will gain a sense of how many action steps or short-term goals are best for your pace so you can stay on track. When one action step is completed, write a new action step. The same goes for each short-term goal. Keep enough pressure on yourself to stay focused on your goals, but not so much pressure that it becomes a burden.

A good example is when you construct a building or house, you must coordinate all the contractors to arrive at the best time for what they will be doing. You don't call the drywall contractor before the electrical and plumbing have been installed. And from experience you have learned not to have the plumber and electrician on site at the same time. They need to work in the same spaces and they tend to get in each other's way. This elevates the tension level, creating more stress.

You will have to be the traffic light and keep the traffic flowing in the right direction at the proper time. If you don't, you may have a wreck on your hands. This means delays, unnecessary adjustments, and loss of valuable resources.

There is nothing here that is set in concrete. You should remain flexible in setting your goals. You should have more than one resource to turn to when you need advice or knowledge regarding each step you take. The purpose is you will be setting loftier goals as you move toward your original goals. This is all part of the evolutionary process and will be influenced by your current environment and circumstances. Adjustments should not be frowned upon since they mean you are at least moving and have recognized the need for a change in direction. If you are not working and reviewing your progress, you may find yourself in the future still wondering if you will ever reach your goal.

Focus on the achievable. Don't be tempted to short-cut any action step or goal. Keep all your time frames achievable also. Don't be guilty of placing unreasonable time constraints on yourself. This will only cause you undue pressure. Do the tests you are most comfortable with to see if your goal or action step is really achievable. An extra couple of minutes can save hours, days, weeks, months, or years of effort being wasted.

Be mindful of opportunities that appear as you achieve your goals. Your awareness will be heightened to what is happening all around you. Take advantage of opportunities that will prove to be a better path for you to take. Also, consider new resources that will come forth and offers of help from unlikely places. Your efforts in working on your goals will pay off more than you can imagine.

> *"Without continual growth and progress, such words as improvement, achievement, and success have no meaning."*
>
> *Benjamin Franklin*

Keep all things in order, one step at a time. It really is the fastest and smoothest path to take to reach your goals.

FOCUS ON THE ACHIEVABLE

It is important to be aware of any potential congested spots along the way. Seeing them ahead of time allows you to make adjustments early so as to avoid any unnecessary delays. Adjustments are part of this process. Don't be discouraged if all is not going as planned. Accept the challenge and make the adjustments. You will be glad you did. You can do this and much more.

In chapter 4, you will learn how to define your plan. You will learn how to use action steps to accomplish your goals. You will be taught about prioritizing your action steps and goals. This is so you can do more in less time.

Looking forward, can you see the success waiting to be achieved?

What's Your Take?

At the end of this chapter you are asked to complete your assignment. You might think of it as a test, quick quiz, or a personal reflection. It will help you see if you understand the material you have read in this chapter. These questions are for you to answer honestly and sincerely.

You have now learned about keeping it simple, keeping it real, and keeping it achievable. These methods have been put to the test over many years. Each step you accomplish will fill your goal setting tool box with the proper tools for success.

Remember, you are responsible for your own success or lack thereof. Don't be looking to hang the blame on someone or something else. You are in charge of you.

Keep moving. Every step toward your goal is progress.

FIVE EASY STEPS TO ACHIEVING YOUR GOALS NOW!

Get Your Notebook

1. Write down one goal you have put to an achievability test.

2. Write one action step that will start you on the path to that goal you have tested.

3. List any obstacles you know of right now that might interfere with achieving the goal.

4. Using one obstacle or obstruction listed above, describe how you might be able to overcome it.

5. Write down the most important concept you learned from this chapter and how it impressed you.

STEP FOUR

Define Your Plan

CHAPTER 4
Define Your Plan

You don't fix the problem until you define it.
John W. Snow

STEP FOUR WILL CONSIST of a total of five chapters. You are now entering the "eye of the storm." Not to worry, it will be safely presented to you. Each chapter will go into more depth in the areas that you will need to consider in preparing your goals.

Chapter 4 will help you understand how to define your plan. Your plan should be without any holes. The action steps are your stepping-stones. They will lead you toward your ultimate goal. All action steps and goals need to be achievable and timely. Prioritize them so you will keep the most important action steps and goals in the forefront.

Define Your Plan

You take shortcuts thinking they will save you time. How often have you asked people for directions and they forgot to mention a turn or two you should have taken? You wasted time getting to your destination. In the end, the shortcut was not that short, and the consequence of not getting accurate information in the first place.

FIVE EASY STEPS TO ACHIEVING YOUR GOALS NOW!

If you took the time to look it up, you would have taken the route more clearly defined. Chances are you would have selected the best route to get to your destination, thus saving yourself some time and frustration.

You need to define in complete detail exactly what you plan to do to get to your goal. If you leave out some important steps or just take off on a tangent, you will not reach your goal within your time frame.

As you lay out your plan, you will see some congested spots and some holes. This is the time to make some adjustments.

By moving some items to other stages or phases you can insert steps to create bridges over gaps in your plan. Some goals will be dependent upon you completing other goals first. Some goals may take time for you to gather the needed information, skills, or knowledge. You will have to get those processes started now so that they will be available when you need them.

> **Remember back in school when the math teacher stated that a problem that is well defined is 80 percent solved? This is true.**
>
> **Remember those math problems not so well defined that we all missed? The devil is in the missing details so give him no quarter. Chase him out by defining your goals in complete detail.**

DEFINE YOUR PLAN

Set Your Stepping-Stones

Consider each action step or goal as a stepping-stone that must be reached in order to achieve your ultimate goal. If you have defined your plan correctly, you will see exactly what you need to do to get to your goal. Sometimes you may have to put in some extra stepping-stones to go around some obstacle or obstruction you encounter along the way. Do not let anything distract you from moving toward your goal.

CASE NOTE

Over the years I have witnessed individuals who got stalled waiting to complete an action step. If something is preventing you from completing an action step and you know it will take some time before you can continue, then start another action step that will keep you moving toward your goals until you can make progress on the delayed action step.

Here is where you will learn about the importance of regularly reviewing how you are progressing. Set aside a few minutes each week to review your progress. Consider a special review as you complete an action step or goal. These reviews will keep you on track and moving in the right direction, and they will provide you an opportunity to make any needed adjustments.

Regularly scheduled times for review will also keep you within your time frame. If something seems to be stalled, you can take action to get it moving. This might involve placing a phone call to a resource who has not yet responded. You have to be proactive and not wait for others. If one resource is not responding, find another one who will. You are responsible for your progress. Don't use outside resources as excuses for your failure to move forward. Take charge of your plan.

Achievable and Timely

Your goals will be achievable if you give them the proper amount of time they need to be completed. Many of us try to force our goals into what we want now. Patience is a real virtue and is, in itself, its own reward. One reason for having patience is it will provide time for an action step to take root and then blossom. Patience will give your efforts time to be proven or help you see what adjustments will be required to keep you on track. Pushing a goal into an unrealistic time frame can cause stress and undesired tension. Discouragement is a real goal-killer. Not finishing a goal within a given time frame is not the end of the world. You might not have known just how long it was going to take to complete the goal when you planned it.

You were presented with the time frames for your goals in chapter 2. For those of you who skipped chapter 2 here they are again. Life goals are those that will take over ten years to complete or realize. Long-term goals are achievable in less than ten years. Medium-term goals are generally completed within two years. Short-term goals are those easily accomplished within six months. And finally, action steps are designed to be achieved within a week or two.

DEFINE YOUR PLAN

Since the action steps are what you will be actively working on in the next week or so, these "mini goals" are what drive you to move toward your ultimate goal. They can be as simple as contacting a resource, doing some research, or sending correspondence by letter, an e-mail, or a phone call. Simple action steps will move you in the direction you want to go.

As you become accustomed to defining your plan and setting each goal in its proper time frame, accomplishing your goals will become much easier. You can see your plan and keep it in order. Defining your plan will make things simple, realistic, and achievable. It will also show what resources and skills you will need, and when they have to be completed to keep you on your time line.

Within your time line, don't forget to include some R&R (rest and recreation). The best time to insert some R&R is after you make some major achievement of one of your goals. Hold the R&R as a carrot to motivate you to reach a point so you can enjoy something special. The time you take for the R&R should be long enough to catch your breath and recharge your energy level so you can keep up the momentum. Don't take too much time, or you will get out of the habit of acting on your goals and they will begin to slip away from you. A short or long weekend is plenty of time for some R&R to get away

> *"Pray that success will not come any faster than you are able to endure it."*
>
> *Elbert Hubbard*

from the grind and the routine, and enjoy life because you have earned it.

Now get back to dedicating your mind to focus on your goals and begin to make progress once again. Working on your goals is a habit and you must strengthen it every day. Remember, it is a privilege and obligation to improve yourself and better your life. You owe it to your family, your community, and the world to improve yourself so you can contribute and give back more than you have taken.

Changes in your behaviors, habits, and accomplishments should be rewarded when achieved. Don't use any excuse to indulge in a reward you have not earned. Success in accomplishing your goal is enough reward. Placing an incentive to get you motivated to achieve your goals is fine as long as you keep it in proper perspective. Enjoy small rewards for the small achievements and big rewards for the major achievements.

Here is a new pledge. Read it aloud. You should read all the pledge cards aloud so you can hear them. Use this pledge to strengthen your goals and make them clearer so your action steps and goals will be easier to achieve. This will help you understand the importance of defining your plan. Take the pledge now also to avoid shortcuts when you define your plan. Define your goals so you can achieve them without distractions, permanent obstructions, or confusion. Defining your goals makes focusing on the important things clearer, sharper, and more achievable.

Be as specific as you can. Keep everything in order and make adjustments when required. Look for weak spots that will impair or hamper your time line. Make sure to be proactive by knowing what will be required and when. Then, have your resources lined up so you can stay on your time line.

> **MY PLEDGE**
> *I will fully define my plan.*
> *I will adhere to my time line and make adjustments when required.*
> *I will enjoy this journey into a new paradigm.*

Get the skills you will need in the beginning. Don't think you will have time later to take care of obtaining the skills, knowledge, or abilities you need now to even start realizing your goal. You crawled before you walked and walked before you ran. The same school of thought applies here. You have to have your foundation properly set in order to build upon it.

As you begin to implement each action step ask yourself if it will really move you toward your goal. If not, look for another action step that will. Don't waste time or effort if it will not help you reach your goal. Avoid distractions that rob you of both time and the opportunities you are seeking.

Review your goals and the progress you are making. If you have defined your plan properly, and you are working on each step, you will be moving toward your goal. It is easy to do a quick check-up. If you see some need for adjustment, you may have to redefine your plan slightly. Better to make slight adjustments now than to return to the beginning and start all over.

Prioritize

Prioritizing is a must. Do what needs to be done first. When you prioritize, you create a more streamlined time line. Things will fall in place and you will be making steady progress toward your goals. You may be required to move things around to make your priority list more efficient. In the long run, it will enable you to get more things done in less time. Saving time is like saving money. It rewards you by allowing you to work on other action steps or goals sooner.

Prioritize what you must do and when. Things will come up daily that require you to change some of your priorities. For example, a resource backs out or does not respond to your requests. Take charge and move on with another resource. Do the important things first. If they are difficult, get them done first and the rest of the day will go much better.

> *"People with clear, written goals accomplish far more in a shorter period of time than people without them could ever imagine."*
> *Brian Tracy*

Always keep your goals in their proper time frame. You should be able to draw a line through each time frame as you complete it and see it move you closer to your ultimate goal. Action steps get you on course to accomplishing your short-term goal. When you achieve your short-term goal you will be even closer

DEFINE YOUR PLAN

to your medium-term goal, long-term goal, and life goal.

Reward yourself when you make a major achievement. Take some R&R. Reward yourself with a cookie or some ice cream when you accomplish an action step. Keep your rewards equal to the weight of the accomplishment. Meeting your life goals is the real reward. The pride and sense of accomplishment and what you are now able to do to help others in your own way is priceless.

How much emphasis you place on each facet will depend mostly on where you are in life. When you are young and in school, your facet regarding self-improvement, which includes education, will take a greater percentage of your focus. To live a balanced life, you still must recognize that the other facets are equally important, but they may not need as much emphasis at this time.

Once you have completed your education, whether it is a degree, a technical or trade school certificate, or specialized vocational training, it doesn't mean you stop learning. Today more than ever before, you have to keep improving your knowledge and skills. You must keep current with the changes in technology and discoveries that change the way things are done. We have witnessed how fast technology has changed our lives, and it is hard to even keep up with all the advancements that are introduced every day.

You are almost there, so stay the course. It will all be worth it as you begin to move toward your goals one step at a time. Reduce your chances for delays or self-imposed stress by reading and studying the next four chapters. They are here to help you define where you are and help you get to where you want to go.

You have learned many things so far. In chapter 5 you will learn about balance. Keeping your life in balance is important. A balanced life helps move you forward in all facets of your life. Don't be guilty of letting one or two facets control your life. Once you have lost control, you begin to lose focus and fall behind on your goals.

Be thankful for all you have and what you will have in the future.

What's Your Take?

At the end of this chapter you are asked to complete your assignment. You might think of it as a test, quick quiz, or a personal reflection. It will help you see if you understand the material you have read in this chapter. These questions are for you to answer honestly and sincerely.

These are your goals. Aim high, lengthen your stride, and look beyond the horizon to see a better tomorrow.

DEFINE YOUR PLAN

Get Your Notebook

1. Take a single short-term goal you will be working on and define completely the plan you will use to achieve it.

2. List any action steps you will need to accomplish before you can begin working on the goal above.

3. List any obstacles you know of right now that might interfere with your being able to begin working on the goal.

4. From the list you made above, pick one obstacle and write how you can overcome it.

5. Write down the most important concept you learned from this chapter and how it impressed you.

STEP FOUR
Continued

Keep Your Balance

CHAPTER 5

Keep Your Balance

There is no decision that we can make that doesn't come with some sort of balance or sacrifice.
Simon Sinek

WITH ALL YOU HAVE to do each day, it's amazing how well you can keep some sort of balance in your life. Balance is great since it allows you to be engaged in many facets of your life without letting one or two facets take over. This is accomplished by keeping all of them in proper perspective and properly weighted.

You will be faced with choices. These choices will require you to make sacrifices. (No, you won't have to give up an arm or a leg. Though once I think there was one who would have given up a kidney to avoid doing one of his action steps.) The sacrifice is giving up the status quo for something better in the future. Due diligence is doing the research you need to do to be better informed. Use the information you have gathered to make informed choices.

Keep Your Balance

Juggling your life with all the demands placed upon it can become a burden if you do not allocate an "importance premium" on each facet. A good juggler can handle many balls, pins, or objects at one time as long as he or she keeps

FIVE EASY STEPS TO ACHIEVING YOUR GOALS NOW!

his or her focus on what is important at the moment.

With goals it is not much different, except you can space your time line to accommodate your goals and put an emphasis on what is the most important goal at a particular time in your life.

You have your vehicle tires balanced so you will have a smooth ride. You ride a bicycle because you have learned how to keep your balance so you won't fall over. A balance pole is used by a high wire artist to balance on the high wire. Extend the pole too much toward one side, and you might tip over to an unwanted and perhaps even fatal fall.

> Dr. Maxwell Maltz (1899–1975) was a plastic surgeon and author. He is best known for his book **Psycho-Cybernetics,** first published in 1960.
>
> He once stated,
>
> ***"Man maintains his balance, poise, and sense of security only as he is moving forward."***

Over the years I have studied various systems of categorizing the facets of life. I found they were expressed in many different terms. Some books on the subject of goals list five facets and others as many as ten facets. After over thirty years writing and teaching goals, I have selected seven facets that I find the easiest to understand and to keep in balance.

This chapter will explain why you need to keep balance

KEEP YOUR BALANCE

in your life. You achieve balance by countering the weight of each facet against the rest. Too much in any one facet without adjustment to the rest will cause you to be off-balance. If you are off-balance you might fall short of achieving your goals.

The facets I selected are universal. They apply to all of us. Everyone can apply the principals associated with each facet to their life. These facets will be described in chapters 6, 7, and 8 in more detail.

The seven facets of our life are:

Health	Family
Spirituality	Self-Improvement
Community	Career
Finances	

Weighting Each Facet

Just how much weight do you give to each facet? This is one of those questions answered by your particular situation. There are many factors to be considered. Age and your current stage in life will have the most influence on how much weight you will give a facet or goal. For example, college students will place the most weight on self-improvement/education. This is because they are in the foundation-building part of their lives. They need knowledge to get better jobs, meet vocational requirements, or obtain skills needed in industry.

Someone who is looking toward retirement in the next five to ten years will put more weight on financial planning and investments. Others might have significant health-related issues that must be addressed. Still others who are starting out and have a growing family will put some extra weight on building family relationships.

We are all different and yet seem to have similar needs during roughly the same phases of our life. The best thing about writing your own goals is that you will be the judge of how much weight you will give to any one facet. You know best your situation and circumstances. You are in the best position to make the call.

By this time you should have filled out the personal inventory summary that can be found in the appendixes of this book. It is also located in the back of the available companion workbook online. The personal inventory summary shows you what you should consider to do first. Remember to do the foundational items first. Don't skip any step. Make sure that you can clearly see where you are now and how to get to where you want to go. It is important that you be honest and realistic about where you are starting from and where you are going. Shortcuts are not allowed. You want to have a solid foundation that can protect you from any setbacks that you might encounter.

Sacrifice

You will have to make some tough choices. You will have to overcome challenges in order to move forward. This means you will have to give up something in order to achieve your goals—at the very least, certainly you will give up time to work on them. You will have to look at the value of the reward versus costs of staying in your current paradigm. If you are planning your goals properly and executing them in a timely manner, you will soon see that the rewards are greater than you had imagined. Change is sometimes the hardest thing you will have to do. If you don't change, you cannot move toward your goal.

Sacrifice in this context means that you will be trading off one thing for something else. For example, you like to watch a show on television every night. Yet, you have the opportunity to improve your skills and knowledge by taking a couple of classes for a few months to get a promotion at work. What do you do? What will have the greatest value or impact on your life? Are you willing to give up some television for a job promotion? Are you willing to sacrifice by saving money and investing in your future? Or do you really need a new super widget that just hit the market?

"Judge your success by what you had to give up in order to get it."

The Dalai Lama

> **CASE NOTE**
>
> While studying for my master of business administration degree, I turned off the television for two hours each night so I could read and study each course. After many months I completed the degree. I was able to catch all the shows that I enjoyed watching when they came back as reruns.
>
> I lost nothing. I gained a degree and still got to see the television shows, only later. I made the choice to do what would provide the greater value and worth in my life. When you look at it this way, the sacrifice was the right thing to do.

There are real choices you will have to make if you truly want to achieve your goals. These sacrifices will be worth the cost to achieve your ultimate goals. You will have to make the choice of staying where you are or moving toward where you want to be. When you sacrifice and put forth the effort in something, it creates additional value. You will increase in personal growth and character. And who can place a price on one's character?

Due Diligence

If you are familiar with investing, you understand the value of doing your due diligence. This is when you look deep into a company to see if it is going to be worth the investment. You will consider the risk-to-reward ratio. Compare this company with the peers in their industry sector. You look to see if this investment is better than taking those funds and putting them into another investment that might have a larger dividend yield. You will read reports, analyze balance sheets, track the market trends, and seek the opinions of financial advisors and brokers. Then you can make an informed decision.

When you are looking for the best deal for a new car, you can spend hours researching who might have the best price, not to mention the exact color you want. This is called doing your due diligence. Comparing nutritional information to determine what is best for you to eat is also doing due diligence. It is the same with setting your goals.

You must know exactly what you will need to get started. And once started, you must know what you will need to sustain your journey toward your goal. Getting it right the first time is important. Know the importance of getting your time frame correct. Ask others how long it took them to reach a similar goal. If you need to take a class, ask how long it will take to finish. If you don't know something, it is hard to make plans. Gather all the information before you start out. Start smart and you will finish even smarter.

Now, make a pledge to keep your life's facets in balance. Each time you look at it in the mirror, read this pledge and each of your other pledges. You will in time see the merit of repeating all these pledges. You will see how important each pledge will be when used in writing your action steps and goals. This will help you understand the meaning of keeping your goals balanced. By keeping things in balance, you can achieve your goals without distractions, permanent obstructions, or confusion. Keeping your goals balanced makes focusing on the important things clearer, sharper, and more doable.

> **MY PLEDGE**
> *I will balance my life's facets.*
> *I will balance my goals.*
> *I will enjoy this journey into a new paradigm.*

Our lives and situations place many demands on us. Without balance, we will create our own obstacles and obstructions in our path toward our goals. Balance is maintained by weighting each facet with the "importance premium" we place on it. The weight is determined by your need to reach your goal along with your current phase in life.

The seven facets of our lives can be balanced. It will take some time and effort to make sure you put the proper emphasis on what you need to do first. Take each step in order and build for value. Each facet is important. One facet should not be left out or you will become unbalanced. You may not feel strongly about the facet regarding the community, but remember your life is impacted by what happens in your community. And the community facet includes county, state, and national issues. Be a good citizen and be knowledgeable about the things your government is doing. Don't wait until it is too late to do anything.

The community facet also includes supporting good causes and organizations that do charitable work. Support those organizations that share your values, or those that tend to do good work in programs, such as volunteers in the libraries or hospitals. You might be one who waits until retirement so you can help an election by being a poll worker before putting very much weight in this facet. That's fine. Do what you can in the meantime to be informed and at least go vote.

"The future that we study and plan for begins today."

Chester O. Fischer

Remember, you will be faced with making some sacrifices. You will exchange some time now for a better tomorrow. Look at the rewards-versus-costs ratio to see what you will gain or lose. All experience is good and even if you do lose, don't lose the lesson. Move forward and don't repeat the things you did wrong the first time.

Take the time to do your due diligence. It takes less time to do the research than to go back and figure out where you went wrong. The lost time and resources could have put you closer to your goal much sooner. Be sure you know exactly what you need and when you will need it. Check your time line and make sure all action steps and goals lead toward your ultimate goal. Don't forget to ask for help. The time to start is now. Tomorrow will be here soon, and if you wait, you will be another day shy of reaching your goal. You are going to be successful in achieving your goals because you are now better prepared to face your challenges.

In chapters 6, 7, and 8 you will be presented with more detailed information about the seven facets of your life. You will gain a better understanding of your responsibilities and how much emphasis you may want to place on each facet of your life.

In chapter 6 you will be introduced to the health and family facets of your life. You will learn that health is important in achieving your goals. The family facet will help you identify resources and support to accomplish your goals.

Life isn't static. If you don't move forward, you are sliding back. Keep moving forward.

What's Your Take?

At the end of this chapter, you are asked to complete your assignment. You might think of it as a test, quick quiz,

FIVE EASY STEPS TO ACHIEVING YOUR GOALS NOW!

or a personal reflection. It will help you see if you understand the material you have read in this chapter. These questions are for you to answer honestly and sincerely.

Success will come from a desire to move forward. Moving forward is what we call success.

KEEP YOUR BALANCE

Get Your Notebook

1. Write down how you plan to balance your life's facets based on your phase in life.

2. Write a statement on how you can use your known resources to help you maintain balance in your life.

3. List any obstacles you know of right now that might interfere with balancing your life's facets.

4. Using one obstacle listed above, describe how you might be able to maintain balance in the other facets to meet this challenge.

5. Write down the most important concept you learned from this chapter and how it impressed you.

STEP FOUR
Continued

Facets of Our Life — Health and Family

CHAPTER 6

Facets of Our Life — Health and Family

*The past, the present and the future
are really one — they are today.*
Harriet Beecher Stowe

THIS CHAPTER WILL DEFINE two of the seven facets of your life. It will give you a better understanding of how each of the facets interfaces with the others. It will give you insight on how you can plan to reach your goals through practical action steps and timing. You can put more of your achieving power into any goal when you use some of the other facets to help you move toward your ultimate goal. You can achieve your goals. You are prepared to meet the challenges and overcome any obstructions you might encounter.

The facets are not listed in any particular order of importance, except health. Without health you will be unable to concentrate on working toward your other goals. You will be preoccupied with the discomfort and manifestations of any illness or health issue. Eat a balanced and healthy diet. Get on a regular exercise program. Get healthy and stay healthy. Make it a priority goal to be well.

Family is your foundation of support. They are always there. Work on your family relationships. Mend any that have been strained in the past and not fully resolved.

FIVE EASY STEPS TO ACHIEVING YOUR GOALS NOW!

Your family relationships are important to help you achieve your goals. Your family wants you to succeed.

Health Facet

The health facet needs your attention every day. Most of us don't give our health much thought until we become unhealthy. How do you write a goal about everyday health? There are so many options on this subject alone, if we addressed each one this book would be several large volumes in length.

> Thomas Carlyle (1795–1881), a Scottish writer, historian, and essayist during the Victorian era, once wrote:
>
> **"He who has health, has hope; and he who has hope, has everything."**

The simplest way to approach goals regarding your health is to question what you eat. Don't worry, I am not going to guilt-trip you about your choices in food. Common sense tells us to eat balanced meals and a variety of foods in moderation to remain healthy. Fast foods once in a while will not harm you, but eating ten hamburgers in a single sitting every day will have some serious consequences in short order.

Since each of us enjoys food from our own culture and from many other cultures, we know we can vary what foods we eat. A varied diet including fruits and vegetables is well known to be a key to good health.

If you know of any deficiencies in your health you are looking at a goal to write down, along with any action steps you will need to achieve your goal. Here is a list of questions offering some food for thought about your health.

When was the last time you saw your doctor? If you can't remember, then one goal will be to get a complete physical with lab tests. Prevention is cheaper than any cure—usually a bit less painful too. A first action step would be to call and make an appointment with your doctor. Once done, you will have achieved a "mini-goal" bringing you closer to your goal of having the physical exam and lab tests.

> *"Time and health are two precious assets that we don't recognize and appreciate until they have been depleted."*
>
> Denis Waitley

The second action step is to be on time for your scheduled appointment with the doctor. After your appointment and the lab tests are completed, you will have to follow up to get the results. Another appointment is another action step. The ultimate goal will not be accomplished until you have been given a clean bill of health from your doctor. If there are any health issues discovered during the physical exam, you may have to create new action steps and goals to correct them.

When was the last time you saw your dentist? Do I have to repeat everything above? I think you know how to do this by now.

Diet

Are you eating a healthy diet? Are you eating in moderation the foods you like? Are you eating a balanced diet? Do you see some action steps and goals in regard to your eating habits?

Exercise

Do you have a regular exercise program? Did you ask the doctor about what sort of exercises he would recommend for someone your age, weight, and condition? Don't overdo any exercise program. If you have a goal to become an Olympic athlete, that is fine. Start out slow and build up to perfection. If you start out too hard too fast, you can actually cause some physical damage to yourself. Taking an evening constitutional walk for a few blocks is far more beneficial than pressing the remote.

Do you know your optimum weight for your body size? What is your blood pressure, and are you within a healthy range for your age and condition? Have you had your eyes examined lately? How is your hearing? Do you have some joint pains that won't go away? Are you getting enough sleep? Is your bed in good condition?

Are you doing mental exercises? There are many things available to give your brain some exercise. Reading is good. Solving math problems is excellent. You might enjoy crossword puzzles, board games, or taking on projects that will require using lots of thought processes to complete.

Keeping the brain in shape is just as important as the physical body.

Once you have identified some health goals, you will need to make them part of your plan. Assign the goals to an appropriate time frame. Create some action steps that take you toward your goal. Scheduling a physical exam should be a very short term goal. It can easily be completed in less than six months, or even less than two months. But it won't happen unless you plan for it to happen. Call and make the appointment. This action step is achievable in less than five minutes.

> *"It is well to be up before daybreak, for such habits contribute to health, wealth, and wisdom."*
>
> Aristotle

If the doctor tells you to lose some weight, let's say fifty pounds, you might want to make this a medium-term goal that you will achieve in less than two years. I am not saying you can't lose fifty pounds in less than six months. But doing it over a longer period of time will allow your body to acclimate to the new you. You will increase your chances of not gaining the weight back when you take a longer time to lose it.

There are thousands of books about improving your health through diet and exercise. Your city library has several shelves' worth of books covering subjects about exercise and healthy eating. With the Internet, you can search many related subjects and get plenty of information. You will find healthy recipes, suggested

FIVE EASY STEPS TO ACHIEVING YOUR GOALS NOW!

physical exercises, and articles related to better health habits to improve the quality of your life.

> **CASE NOTE**
>
> After I had some surgery I wanted to get back to exercising as soon as I could. I thought I was ready, but my body told me I was not ready. If there are some medical issues requiring surgery to correct, be sure to consult with your doctor or doctors. You will need to adequately put not only the surgery into your plan, but also the required recovery time. Make sure you are ready to get back to exercising. Some surgery may cause you to delay some goals, and you will have to adjust your time frames accordingly.

When you lose your health, it will impact your ability to work. If you can't work, you can't pay your bills. When you can't pay your bills, you will increase your stress and anxiety levels. In turn, this will cause additional health issues making it harder to get better.

Unfortunately accidents do happen, and never at an opportune time. An accident will have a significant impact on your goals. You will have to make some major adjustments. You will have to prioritize your goals and their time frames so they remain realistic. Life happens, and we have to deal with it. Some things we just cannot control. However, we can manage how we deal with the situation.

You know that working on an exercise program will improve your health. Learning how to prepare and eat healthy foods will be worth the effort at any age. Educate yourself about your health, and when you visit the doctor, you will be able to ask better questions and get more out of the appointment.

Of the seven facets the health facet is the one with the most influence over the others. If you are sick and cannot work on your goals then you are moving away from accomplishing them. Stay fit, and stay healthy.

Family Facet

Family relationships are the motivating factors for us to go to work and to move forward. You go to work so you can provide for your family and meet their needs. Family is a very broad term, with many definitions. No matter who you are, you are a part of a family. You are a son, a daughter, a brother, a sister, an aunt, an uncle, a father, a mother, a husband, a wife, or a grandparent. You may be part of a highly cohesive functional family or a member of a dysfunctional family. You are still a member of a family.

> *"No other success [in life] can compensate for failure in the home."*
> *David O. McKay*

The term can also be extended to include your neighborhood family, your church family, or any organization you belong to. Families today have different structures and norms from past generations. Belonging to something that offers support and comfort combined with a sense of being gives our lives a meaningful purpose.

Relationships

Family is definitely about relationships. How you interact with other members of your family is important. How they perceive you and how you feel about them introduces emotional elements into your life. And how strong or strained these relationships are will have an impact on your performance regarding the other facets.

Here are some questions you will need to consider in establishing your family goals. What are your relationships with other members of your family? Can you improve or strengthen those relationships? Are there any relationships that have been damaged or hurt that are in need of repair? What can you do to rectify these situations? Do you have a communication issue with any family members? How can you correct this deficiency? Can you schedule some family time? Will you be able to spend some time with individual members of the family? Are you planning a family vacation or some family activities in the near future?

"Treasure your relationships, not your possessions."

Anthony J. D'Angelo

If nothing else, a family is always there for you. Your best supporters are those family members who know you can accomplish your goals. This is one reason you should repair every strained family relationship. As you work on your goals, you will need family support. If left unresolved, some negative feelings with family members might hold you back.

Reaching out can be the hardest part of repairing family relationships. Yet these action steps and goals are quick and easy to accomplish. You might be surprised to find that the other family member has been just as unsure about how to approach you. Once you make your peace offering, you will wonder why it took you so long to take any action. As you fix these relationships, you will have a great emotional sense of accomplishment. Don't be surprised if later on you consider these mended relationships some of your greatest achievements.

Your health is very important. Everything else in life revolves around how you feel. Have regular visits with your doctor, dentist, and eye doctor. Eat healthy meals and become knowledgeable about the foods you should include in your diet. Eat in moderation. Remember, fresh is best.

Exercise according to the program you and your doctor have agreed on. Get to your desired weight and maintain it. Don't forget to do mental exercises to keep your mind in shape. Get a good night's sleep. Wake up refreshed and ready to go.

You are a member of a family. Somewhere you do fit in. This is where your center of support comes from. Improve your relationships. All relationships can be improved. Make amends with those with whom you have a strained relationship. Work to make things right.

FIVE EASY STEPS TO ACHIEVING YOUR GOALS NOW!

In chapter 7 more facets will be presented and discussed. These will be the spirituality, self-improvement (or education), and community facets. All facets need to be balanced. You are doing great! Only a few more chapters and your life will be changed forever.

Everyday, express your gratitude to those who have helped you move forward.

What's Your Take?

At the end of the next few chapters there will be some changes made. I want you to take some time and give some thought to how you will apply what you have learned in this chapter. What you write will be the foundation for some of your goals.

Keep working daily to improve. Never lower your standards. Take pride in your transformation.

FACETS OF OUR LIFE — HEALTH AND FAMILY

Get Your Notebook

1. Write down how you plan to take care of your health facet.

2. Write a goal that will help you execute the above plan.

3. Write an action step to begin your journey toward accomplishing a health facet goal.

4. Write down an obstacle that you might face in your health facet and how you might overcome this obstruction.

5. Write down the most important concept you learned from this chapter about your health facet and how it impressed you.

6. Write down how you plan to take care of your family facet.

7. Write a goal that will help you execute the above plan.

8. Write an action step to begin your journey toward accomplishing a family facet goal.

9. Write down an obstacle that you might face in your family facet and how you might overcome this obstruction.

FIVE EASY STEPS TO ACHIEVING YOUR GOALS NOW!

10. Write down the most important concept you learned from this chapter about your family facet and how it impressed you.

STEP FOUR
Continued

Facets of Our Life — Spirituality, Self-Improvement, and Community

CHAPTER 7

Facets of Our Life — Spirituality, Self-Improvement, and Community

*Striving for success without hard work is like trying
to harvest where you haven't planted.*
David Bly

THIS CHAPTER WILL DEFINE three more of the seven facets of your life. The facets presented in this chapter will integrate well with the two facets presented in chapter 6.

While there will be some who do not believe in a higher power, there are many more who believe there is something much greater than we are. Some individuals may not put stock into spiritual goals and I respect their views. I only know spiritual goals have played a role in my life. They have also influenced the lives of many individuals I have known, no matter what faith they belonged to. Remember, we are talking about keeping balance in your life, and spirituality is one facet to be considered to maintain your equilibrium.

Self-improvement is another way to say education. Once you have the education required for your vocation, you will still be expected to keep your skills and abilities sharp. Also consider that self-improvement includes perfecting your avocation and hobby interests. Life is one big learning opportunity, and you should take full advantage to become a better and more informed individual.

Community seems to be the most overlooked of all the facets of your life. This is all about being part of the solution rather than part of the problem. Being informed about what is going on locally, statewide, or nationally is important. Do not let the political advertisements tell you how to vote. Read and study the actual propositions or issues, learn about each candidate, and come to your own conclusions. If more of us did this, we would not have so much uncertainty in the world today.

Spirituality Facet

Spirituality is, to some, a very touchy subject. For some it is a very deep and private matter. For others, it is a public way of life. No matter where you are spiritually, it is between you and your maker. I don't have the right to challenge you about your beliefs or feelings about any particular religious doctrine or philosophical leanings. I do however, expect others to show the same respect for my views and beliefs. If nothing else, on this subject we can agree to disagree. Many individuals look toward a higher power for direction and meaning in their lives, and they seem to find it.

> Ralph Waldo Emerson is quoted as saying,
>
> **"Great men are they who see that spiritual is stronger than any material force — that thoughts rule the world."**

There are many religions that play an important part

SPIRITUALITY — SELF-IMPROVEMENT — COMMUNITY

in how societies rule themselves. When you become a member of a church, synagogue, or mosque, you should learn all you can to be a better member of the congregation. I do not suggest you run out and join any church hoping to increase your spirituality. Find one that meets your needs and makes you feel comfortable and welcomed.

You may be asking yourself what some spiritual goals are. Some are simple, such as "attend your church on a regular basis." Others might be a bit more complex, like trying to find the meaning of life. (In my opinion, the meaning of life is to live it the best you can and to share what you can with others in need.)

> **"In order to experience everyday spirituality, we need to remember that we are spiritual beings spending some time in a human body."**
>
> *Barbara de Angelis*

Here are several questions you can ask yourself to give you some ideas for your spiritual goals. How is your relationship with your Heavenly Father? How well do you know the scriptures? Are you attending and participating in church activities? Are there any books you would like to read to help increase your spirituality? Have you offered your services to help those less fortunate than you? Do you pay a full tithe on the money you earn? Are you generous in your giving toward viable charities?

Have you let the church leaders know you would like to teach, so you can learn more by preparing the lessons? Are you interested in being on a committee to help plan activities to bring members closer together socially? Do you have your own copies of the books and materials needed to help you?

Certainly there are many more questions you can ask. You can ask your church leaders for additional suggestions. Ask your friends who attend church for some ideas. If you look around you will find many opportunities that you can turn into action steps and goals. You can choose to pray for help and guidance. Whatever your choice is, do it with all your heart.

Self-Improvement/Education Facet

For years I have taught a simple principal: "You pay for education once, but you will pay for ignorance every day of your life."

You spend a good portion of life being educated. What you do with it depends on your motivation. Education, knowledge, and your own experiences are part of your personal value. It is this value you take with you when looking for a new job or seeking a promotion.

"Some people drink from the fountain of knowledge, others just gargle."

Robert Anthony

Education is not just limited to a formal classroom setting. It can happen anywhere at any time. It can be one-on-one with a mentor. It can involve studying to be an apprentice for a vocational or technical trade. Learning a skill or trade early in life will be the greatest gift you can give yourself. Many have waited until it was too late. The cost in time and money may not be a good return on the investment you make in a later phase of your life.

Don't wait until it is too late to get the education you need. Get it now, so you can move forward.

Remember when we discussed realistic goals in chapter 2? Here are some ideas you might consider as possible goals for self-improvement and education.

CASE NOTE

I have worked with many individuals who are in their late fifties or early sixties and want to pursue a vocation that requires a skill set geared for someone in their twenties or thirties. By the time they acquire the education, skills, and abilities to do the job, they will be looking at retirement.

Plan your life according to where you are now and where you might be when you have what it takes to obtain your dream job. If you start medical school at age forty-five, the odds that you will be a good surgeon are not in your favor.

What knowledge or skill can I learn to merit a promotion at work? How can I improve my speaking and communication skills? Do I read the right books and magazines to help improve myself in the direction I would like to go? Do I need to learn another language? Can I save money by learning to do minor auto repairs myself? How can I learn more about a hobby that interests me?

FIVE EASY STEPS TO ACHIEVING YOUR GOALS NOW!

You know that working on an exercise program will improve your health. Learning how to prepare and eat healthy foods will be worth the effort at any age. Educate yourself about your health, and when you visit the doctor, you will be able to ask better questions and get more out of the appointment.

Over the years, from my observations, there have been two main obstacles preventing individuals from moving forward in their lives. These are education and language. Education is a problem if you do not have a GED or a high school diploma. This basic education level is achievable if you make the effort. Going for a certificate or a degree is possible for everyone. Language can be a disadvantage if you speak in a foreign tongue and lack the English language skills needed to be successful in the United States. Even so, I have known several individuals who spoke English as their first and only language who had issues of communicating.

Be honest with yourself. You know if you need to improve your skills and knowledge. You have to give yourself a chance for a better life. This has to be a high priority for any goals you set. Ask for help. Ask those who have jobs you think you might enjoy. Talk to them about the knowledge, education, and skill set required.

It might look like it will take a long time, but once you start making progress, you will be closer to your ultimate goals. If you don't take the first step, it won't matter how long the path is, because you will never see what's at the other end. Every day you delay getting the knowledge and education you need, you put off reaching your goals by an equal amount.

Community Facet

We are all members of a community, whether we are participating or non-participating. Part of your civic duty is to be aware of what is going on at all levels of government. From the local city council to the halls of Congress, you should be well-informed as to what they are doing. More rules and regulations are being written daily. More government entities are taking more in taxes and offering less service. Your voice counts, so let them know how you feel.

Some communities are now going into bankruptcy. They have been mismanaged without the community knowing what they were doing. By the time the citizens realize what has happened, it is usually too late to correct the problem.

> *"In doing what we ought we deserve no praise, because it is our duty."*
>
> *Saint Augustine*

Being knowledgeable about the issues and where the candidates stand on them is your responsibility. You have an obligation you need to take seriously. When you get the voters' ballot booklet, take time to read it. Understand the issues to be decided on Election Day.

Consider the following when you are setting goals about the community facet. Set a goal to read the voters' pamphlet and understand the issues and the candidates' views. Make it a goal to vote in every election, no matter how small or large. Is there a worthy cause or organization you should support to help improve your community? Should you volunteer to help the local library or hospital? Can you help out the local food bank? Will you help those in need by supporting a community outreach program with your time and treasure? Is there a community clean-up scheduled in which you can participate? Is there a neighborhood watch program or can one be established on the street where you live?

There are many worthy organizations serving the youth and seniors in your community. Find out what they are doing and see if you can help them continue to make your community a better place to live. If your community has a local theater, you may be able to help them as a volunteer with your skills and talents. Don't be afraid to do your part.

Whatever your faith or your religious affiliation is, it influences your perspectives on life. Spirituality is your own inner peace or refuge from the pressures of the world. It is an important facet and should be given its due when you are setting your goals.

Life has been called an education. You are a living and learning being. When learning ceases, life begins to fade. Challenge yourself to learn something new every day. You will not regret the time invested.

Belonging to a community, you have a responsibility to be informed. Know what the local government is doing. Be informed of the issues that will impact your life. Serve where you can to make your community a better place to live.

You can now see how your goals work together in bringing about a better you. Each facet is part of the whole. Take one away and you greatly reduce your chances for changing your life. You will accomplish your goals. You are building a solid foundation on which to build a better life for you, your family, and your community.

In chapter 8 you will learn about the final two facets. You will see how your career and finance facets complement the facets you have learned about in the previous chapters.

The further up the trail you go, the less crowded and easier it becomes.

What's Your Take?

Take some time and give some thought to how you will apply what you have learned in this chapter. What you write will be the foundation for some of your goals.

Your attitude will move you forward faster when it is positive. Don't let a negative attitude hold you back.

FIVE EASY STEPS TO ACHIEVING YOUR GOALS NOW!

Get Your Notebook

1. Write down how you plan to take care of your spirituality facet.

2. Write a goal that will help you execute the above plan.

3. Write an action step to begin your journey toward accomplishing a spirituality facet goal.

4. Write down a priority list of some of your spirituality facet goals and create an appropriate time line for each.

5. Write down the most important concept you learned from this chapter about your spirituality facet and how it impressed you.

6. Write down how you plan to take care of your self- improvement or educational facet.

7. Write down a priority list of some of your self-improvement facet goals and create an appropriate time line for each.

8. Write an action step that you will need to turn the plan written above into reality.

9. Write down any obstructions that might keep you from accomplishing your action steps or goals regarding self-improvement or education.

10. Write down the most important concept you learned from this chapter about your self-improvement facet and how it impressed you.

11. Write down how you plan to take care of your community facet.

12. Write a goal that will help you execute the above plan.

13. Write an action step to begin your journey toward accomplishing a community facet goal.

14. Write down a priority list of some of your community facet goals and create an appropriate time line for each.

15. Write down the most important concept you learned from this chapter about your community facet and how it impressed you.

STEP FOUR
Continued

Facets of Our Life — Career and Finances

CHAPTER 8

Facets of Our Life — Career and Finances

You can have financial strength, professional strength, emotional strength but for me without spiritual strength none of the rest of it matters.
Star Jones

THIS CHAPTER WILL DEFINE the last two facets of your life. Most might think these two should have been the first facets presented. These are the two facets on which most individuals place the most importance. The reason they have been held back to the end is simple. All facets are important. While you might think a measure of success must be either a professional title or a financial status, you might be wrong.

Edward H. Harriman once stated,

"Every man should make up his mind that if he expects to succeed, he must give an honest return for the other man's dollar."

The measure of success is what you think about your particular situation or circumstance and your willingness to accept whatever it is. Contentment and the enjoyment of the simple pleasures of life are in reality the embodiment of success.

All honest and honorable work is to be respected. We should be honest in any profession in which we choose to work. Be the best you can be. Don't settle for anything less. Take pride in your work.

The prisons are filled with those less than honest and without honor, and they come from all professions and financial strata. Don't look down on someone who has a lesser education or title. If you limit your association to only those who are your equals professionally or financially, you are missing out on some of the most rewarding experiences life has to offer. Try to learn something from everyone you meet. Let them enrich your soul as you inspire them to move forward in their life.

Your financial facet is one of the most important facets. Understand how to budget and understand how money works. Having money is all about the freedom to do what you really want to do. Money is only a tool and like any tool it can be used to build or to demolish. How you choose to use your financial knowledge will be rewarded with its own consequences.

Career Facet

This facet deals with your choice of career, which is very important. It will have an impact on all your other facets. You will spend your working years hopefully doing what you enjoy. If not, you will be changing jobs and careers, and be ultimately frustrated. Each time you start over, you actually lose some ground. If the new career proves to be a better and more rewarding one, you can regain some of the loss. If it doesn't, then you will be back at square one wondering what to do next.

> **CASE NOTE**
>
> I have known many who thought they would really enjoy a certain career. They spent plenty of time and money to pursue it, only to get into the profession and realize it was not what they originally thought it was. They found that the job required more of their time, and the expectations of the organization went beyond what they had been led to believe.

There are many things one must consider when researching a career or profession. Some things might be viewed as perks. Ask yourself some of the following questions and see if they are really worth the trade-offs.

How much time will you be required to be away from home? Are you willing to relocate? Will your family be happy with the demands the job will require of you? Do you want to travel and live out of a suitcase for days, weeks, or months? Will you have any input as to where you will go, and when?

Certainly these are not the only questions that can be asked. And for some, these questions are not that important. Take the time to discuss the positives and negatives about any career move you might be considering. Choices come with consequences, good or bad, and they will have repercussions affecting others whose interests you should take into consideration.

If you seek to find people who are happy in what they do for a living, you might find those in lower-paying jobs the happiest. Why? For one reason, they don't take on as much responsibility. Their jobs are fairly routine and not complicated. On the other hand, those who seek more challenging vocations can handle stress and pressure better. Some like the responsibility of managing complicated projects, coordinating suppliers, materials, and time schedules. Others enjoy just being told what to do and when.

We all have seen the "lemmings" that have followed whatever was the latest job fad. One friend finds a job and invites everyone they know to apply. A few might work out. The majority will soon be gone in search of something else.

> *"An unfulfilled vocation drains the color from a man's entire existence."*
>
> Honore de Balzac

I do know experience is valuable. Not all experience is transferable from one career to another. Those who cultivate good people skills will find this is not only a transferable but a highly sought trait most employers are looking for. It is also very valuable if you are self-employed.

Once you have decided to pursue a particular career, you will need to research what skills, talents, abilities, and knowledge will be required. Some vocations require a few months of technical training and certification. Others require a degree that might take several years to accomplish. Some jobs only require some muscle and an ability to take direction and understand basic instructions.

Life happens, and a career you thought would be there for as long as you planned to work can suddenly vanish. Companies go out of business, or they merge with one another, and many suffer from the downsizing that follows. Always have a Plan B, or at least have some skills where there will always be a market.

> *"When you become famous, being famous becomes your profession."*
> *James Carville*

No matter what vocation or career you find yourself in, be passionate in doing your best at all times. Doing your best at something you enjoy is not considered work. It is called life. Enjoy what you do and it will be noticed, if by none other than yourself.

Finances Facet

Financial status is one measure of how an individual may be perceived, though in reality, true success involves far more than just one's financial statement. The financial facet, if not diligently worked on, can ruin all your goals, dreams, and desires. Therefore, you will require some basic knowledge about money, budgets, and investments.

Fear not, for there are plenty of resources available to assist you. Just be careful of who they are and why they want to offer you help. There are plenty of good financial resources. They are not hard to find, and they will cost little, or even nothing.

One of the most basic elements of being financially fit is having a budget. It is not necessary to have one as large as the national budget. A simple budget is the best—easy to read, easy to follow, and easy to change as needed.

FIVE EASY STEPS TO ACHIEVING YOUR GOALS NOW!

Simply list your expenses and your income and do some addition and subtraction, and you will see how much is left over. There are those who like to go deeper into analyzing all expenditures and determining how to lower the percentage they take away from all sources of income. If you can work with a more complex budget, then do it. The point is, everyone needs to understand what a basic budget is and how to use it. In the appendixes you will find a simple budget worksheet for your use if you do not have one.

> *"Pursuing your passion is fulfilling and leads to financial freedom."*
>
> Robert G. Allen

For most of our lives, we are very dependent on the wages we earn from our jobs. Multiple streams of income are not yet on our radar, let alone investing in stocks, precious metals, or bonds. There should come a time, though, when you realize that Social Security and that 401k might fall short of what you will need to live on in retirement. Hopefully you will reach this realization sooner rather than later.

The financial facet is one you must deal with your entire life. From the first allowance you received as a child, you began dealing with finances. Those who learn how to deal with money and how money works will make the most of it. Those who don't won't have to worry about it, since there won't be any money to worry about!

When planning any goal, know exactly what will be needed and then budget for it. As you begin to map out your plan, you will see obstacles that will need to be overcome.

For example, say you lack the educational requirement for the position at work you had always dreamed of having. Obtaining this education will require a financial investment that you will have to include in your budget. Don't forget that you will also have to budget enough time to accomplish the goal.

You might be thinking that time should be considered an eighth facet. The reason it is not is because time was given to us to manage. It is given to all in the same measure. We can control it by how we utilize and budget time for our own purposes. Use it wisely, for it cannot be carried over to another day.

> *"I finally know what distinguishes man from the other beasts: financial worries."*
>
> Jules Renard

The financial facet will utilize time frames a bit more than the other facets. Action steps might require the purchase or enrollment costs of pursuing knowledge. A short-term goal might require costs associated with travel or correspondence to move toward your medium-term or longer-term goals. Buying a new car might be one of your long-term goals, five years might be your target date. Figure out what you will have to save or set aside, including an inflationary factor. This will provide the funds you will need at the proper time and in the then-current dollar value.

You will have to plan your financial facet to include what you will need and want, and what might intrude into your life. You know prudent financial planning includes a rainy day fund for the unexpected. We know it will happen, we just don't know when—only that it will be at the most inopportune time. Nevertheless, you must be prepared for all contingencies.

What you choose to do to earn money is up to you. You should pick a job or career that you will enjoy. Pick one where you can make a difference in your life and the lives of others. Study and train for the job and do your best. Be honorable and always set the example of integrity and character.

Know your finances at all times. Work out your budget and know where you are spending your money. Don't leave anything to chance. The more you know about how money works, the more money will work for you. It is not about how much you spend, but how much you keep that counts.

Chapter 9 is all about taking action. All your plans, dreams, desires, and aspirations are meaningless unless you take action. Now you have all the tools to create a plan. You are now ready to take action. You are going to be successful. You will enjoy the journey.

Appreciate the simple pleasures of life. Success and accomplishment are two simple pleasures you are entitled to earn.

What's Your Take?

I want you to take some time and give some thought to how you will apply what you have learned in this chapter. What you write will be the foundation for some of your goals. Keep it simple, realistic, achievable, well-defined, and balanced so you can achieve your goals. You now have the seven facets, and it is up to you to move forward.

FACETS OF OUR LIFE — CAREER AND FINANCES

Time will not pause or wait. You must keep up with it or it will be gone without any progress toward your goal.

FIVE EASY STEPS TO ACHIEVING YOUR GOALS NOW!

Get Your Notebook

1. Write down how you plan to take care of your career facet.

2. Write a goal that will help you execute the above plan.

3. Write an action step to begin your journey toward accomplishing a career facet goal.

4. Write down a priority list of some of your career facet goals and create an appropriate time line for each.

5. Write down the most important concept you learned from this chapter about your career facet and how it impressed you.

6. Write down how you plan to take care of your finances facet.

7. Write down a priority list of some of your finances facet goals and create an appropriate time line for each.

8. Write an action step that you will need to turn the written plan above into reality.

9. Write down any obstacle or obstruction that might hinder you in accomplishing your finance goals at this time.

10. Write down the most important concept you learned from this chapter about your financial facet and how it impressed you.

STEP FIVE

Take Action

CHAPTER 9

Take Action

Nothing is so fatiguing as the eternal hanging on of an uncompleted task.
Benjamin Disraeli

LIKE THE REST OF you, I find planning and research to be the easy part of setting goals. Just take some paper, put down a few things I would like to accomplish, and I am done. Well, preparation is only a part of the goal. Taking action is perhaps the hardest part. Why? Because we have a fear of change and the unknown, and some doubt regarding our ability to see our actions through to achievement.

> William M. Winans (1788–1857) was one of the pioneers of Methodism in Mississippi. He was a clergyman and circuit rider. He is best known for this observation:
>
> **"Not doing more than the average is what keeps the average down."**

You now have the knowledge and resources at hand to set your goals properly. What you have done is assembled a goal setting tool box. Look inside your tool box and you will find the tools to simplify and define your goals. Other tools include the knowledge of how to make your goals realistic and achievable. You will also find the tools to measure your accomplishments. Look deeper into the tool box and you will find tools that are the individuals and resources to help you move toward your goals.

So look in your mirror and say, "It is time to take action *now!*" The fact that you have read this far, shows you are above average. You want to move to a new paradigm and you are willing to take on the challenge. That's great! No more excuses. Remember, excuses are not acceptable. Excuses are a sign of poor planning, lack of prioritization, and laziness. Do yourself proud. Take action now. Let the journey begin. Enjoy the ride.

Take Action Now

Here is where you begin. You should have a rough draft of some goal ideas. Some of your goals should have been written down as the assignment at the end of each chapter's "What's your take?" To start, pick one goal, build a time line, and create some action steps that will move you toward your goal. Be sure to utilize all the tools you have been taught. This is the time when your learning morphs into your action. Make the action steps easy enough to accomplish within one to two weeks. Don't take on too much too soon. Remember, it is one step at a time.

Taking action is a big part of goal setting. A very simple goal complete with time line, action steps, and possible adjustments will be presented in this chapter. This is a schedule or an agenda you could use by substituting your own action steps and goals.

TAKE ACTION

The time line begins on Sunday, June 15, for a short-term goal to lose fifteen pounds by Monday, December 15. Note how the goal is written and defined. Each action step takes you one step closer to your ultimate goal. At one point in the time line, you will be required to make some adjustments. Take note on how they are handled to get you back on track.

Nothing will happen unless you plan to take action and then do it. Wishing and hoping will not make it happen. You are in charge of your life. Take control and be diligent in your efforts. You are capable of accomplishing your goals when you take action to do so.

> *"Just remember, you can do anything you set your mind to, but it takes action, perseverance, and facing your fears."*
>
> *Gillian Anderson*

CASE NOTE

For those who have never set goals before, my recommendation is to work on one short-term goal with several action steps that will culminate in the achievement of that goal. With the taste of success from accomplishing the goal, you will begin to lose your fear of change. You will then have proved to yourself that you can do it. We knew you could!

In the next several paragraphs, a simple goal will be defined and planned out. Take the time to read it. It will help you understand how simple goal setting can be.

FIVE EASY STEPS TO ACHIEVING YOUR GOALS NOW!

The goals and action steps will be in **bold** type. The time line will be in the regular type. A running commentary will be in *italic* type. This will allow you to better understand the thought processes behind how the goal will be accomplished within six months.

> **PLEASE NOTE** the following is presented for illustration purposes only. Before doing any exercise program or making any changes to your diet, see your medical professional for advice.

Sunday, June 15   **Goal: To improve my health and become more physically fit. I want to lose fifteen pounds by Monday, December 15. I want to improve my diet by eating healthier foods and begin a low- impact exercise program.**

Here, the health facet has been selected and the desired results have been defined. The amount of weight to be lost is clear, and a firm, realistic target date is established. A low-impact exercise program should be discussed with your physician to make sure that you are fit enough for your goal. The doctor can also give some advice on how to improve your diet.

Sunday, June 15   **Action Step 1: Call doctor to set up an appointment. To be completed by Wednesday, June 18.**

TAKE ACTION

> **Action Step 2: Go to library and check out two healthy eating cookbooks. To be completed by Friday, June 20.**

Wait a minute! What's he doing with two action steps at the same time? You will find that many action steps can be done concurrently. Action steps are bite-sized and can have different objectives that will not conflict in scope or time. For example, calling the doctor's office to set up an appointment is not a three-day project. Take a couple of minutes and just make the call. Going to the library to check out some books on healthy eating might be completed on any day while driving any errand that takes you by the library.

You have only set a target date for when the action step must be completed. You can always complete any action step prior to the target date. By doing so, you will be moving your time line closer to reaching your goal. The only exception is when you have a set appointment with someone. Then, make sure you keep the appointment as scheduled.

By completing your action steps on or before their target date, you will be holding yourself accountable. The minute you complete an action step, set the next one. Keep the momentum going!

In the example here, you called the doctor on Monday, June 16, and the doctor's office has scheduled you for Wednesday, June 25, at 10:00 a.m.

Monday, June 16 | **Action Step 3: Keep the appointment at the doctor's office at 10:00 a.m. Wednesday, June 25.**

FIVE EASY STEPS TO ACHIEVING YOUR GOALS NOW!

You managed to get to the library on Thursday, June 19, and checked out the two healthy eating cookbooks.

Thursday, June 19   **Action Step 4: Read one healthy eating cookbook by Monday, June 23.**

The cookbook was so good, you finished reading it Sunday, June 22, ahead of the scheduled target completion date.

Sunday, June 22   Review progress to date.

Action Step 5: Read the second healthy eating cookbook by Friday, June 27.

Ah! Sunday night, June 22: take a few minutes to review your progress to date. You have completed three action steps in the first week. Congratulations! Now review your open action steps to see if there are any obstacles that might interfere with you completing them as scheduled.

You kept the doctor's appointment as scheduled on Wednesday, June 25. The doctor stated he found nothing that should prevent you from implementing a moderate exercise program of walking and gave some suggestions about diet modification. He suggested for the first two weeks, you walk every other day for fifteen minutes. After two weeks, you can increase the walk to thirty minutes every other day.

TAKE ACTION

Wednesday, June 25

Action Step 6: Walk for fifteen minutes every other day for two weeks, starting on Wednesday, June 25. To be completed on Monday, July 7.

Action Step 7: Plan two weeks of menus reducing fat and carbohydrates by 25 percent daily. Begin to serve them starting on Thursday, June 26.

Here you are, off to a great start. Remember, you will have to set aside time weekly for when you will review your progress and reevaluate your action steps and goals. Sunday night is good, since it will help you focus on the upcoming week. Some may feel it best to have an action step for the weekly review. If you want to have an action step to remind you, that's fine.

Also, be sure to have a scale so you can track your weight loss. Your baseline weight should be what the doctor's office recorded. You should have made a follow-up appointment for Monday, December 15, while you were still at the doctor's office. If you did not make a future appointment, set a goal at a later date to call the doctor and make the follow-up appointment.

After a few weeks, you can take a look at your menus. You might want to keep a couple of meals that you enjoy and insert a few new ones to try out. If you have enlisted or drafted your family to join you in the foods you are eating, you might get some feedback from them. You will need their support, and you do not want to give cause for a mutiny.

FIVE EASY STEPS TO ACHIEVING YOUR GOALS NOW!

Sunday, June 29 — Review progress, action steps, and goals, and record weight.

Sunday, July 6 — Review progress, action steps, and goals, and record weight.

Monday, July 7 has arrived, and so you have completed your fifteen-minute walking assignments. Time for another action step.

Tuesday, July 8 — **Action Step 8: Increase walking time to thirty minutes every other day starting on Wednesday, July 9.**

Sunday, July 13 — Review progress, action steps, and goals, and record weight.

Thursday, July 17 — **Action Step 9: Plan new menus keeping those that you enjoyed the most and introducing some new ones for variety. Begin new menu on Friday, July 18.**

Sunday, July 20 — Review progress, action steps, and goals, and record weight.

Each week, you should see some weight reduction. Since everyone is different, the amount of weight lost will be different.

TAKE ACTION

At this point, you will be about a month into the six months you have set as your target date to reach your goal. You are feeling more fit and have an increased energy level. So you feel like you want to add an extra day of walking thirty minutes each week, time to write a new action step.

Sunday, July 20	**Action Step 10: Walk for thirty minutes one more day per week starting today.**
Sunday, July 27	Review progress, action steps, and goals, and record weight.
Sunday, August 3	Review progress, action steps, and goals, and record weight.
Sunday, August 10	Review progress, action steps, and goals, and record weight.

It is finally here! No, it is not the completion of your goal. It is the two week family vacation at Grandma's house. What do you do about keeping up with your action steps and your Sunday reviews? Not to worry. You can still take your thirty minute walks every other day. If there is a scale, you can still record your progress. So, things are not so bad. However, Grandma's cooking will be a challenge. Not that she is a bad cook; in fact, she is a great cook, famous for her decadent and sinfully rich chocolate desserts.

Your Sunday reviews reveal that some of your lost weight has somehow found its way back to you. We know that you didn't

FIVE EASY STEPS TO ACHIEVING YOUR GOALS NOW!

go looking for it. Now you have to make some adjustments when you get home.

Sunday, August 24 — Review progress, action steps, and goals, and record weight.

Action Step 11: Increase thirty minute walks to six days per week. Begin this action step on Monday, August 25.

Action Step 12: Make changes to weekly menus again. Keep several favorites and introduce some new ones that are lower in calories, fat, and carbohydrates. Begin new menu on Wednesday, August 27.

These changes are not as drastic as you might think. They are merely some minor adjustments to get you back on course. The extra days of walking will burn off more weight, and the reduced calories, fat, and carbohydrates will also help shed some extra weight.

Sunday, August 31 — Review progress, action steps, and goals, and record weight.

Sunday, September 7 — Review progress, action steps, and goals, and record weight.

TAKE ACTION

Sunday, September 14   Review progress, action steps, and goals, and record weight.

On Monday, September 15, you will have reached the midpoint of your six month goal. Your results show that you have lost about half the weight you have set as your goal, so you are doing fine. Keep up the good work!

Monday, September 15   **Action Step 13: Verify (or make) the doctor's appointment for Monday, December 15, for a follow-up check-up, to be completed by Friday, September 19.**

By now, you should have a feel for how this all works. You might want to add another action step or two to change the menus to keep them fresh. On Monday, December 1, you will need another action step to keep the appointment you have scheduled for Monday, December 15.

Monday, December 1   **Action Step 14: Keep the doctor's appointment you scheduled for 10:30 a.m. on Monday, December 15.**

This is how you take action. Commit yourself to the goal and create action steps that will lead to achievement within the time frame you have set. Keep yourself accountable for your weekly progress reviews. If there are obstacles in your path, find a way to go around them or eliminate them if possible.

FIVE EASY STEPS TO ACHIEVING YOUR GOALS NOW!

By maintaining a regular schedule for review, you are setting up a cadence of accountability. You will develop this routine in order to see how well you are doing and holding yourself accountable for your progress. Get into the habit of reviewing your action steps and goals each week. It is important to have regular time scheduled so you can be sure to put it on your calendar or set an alarm to notify you that you have an appointment with yourself to review your plan.

Chapter 10 will help you understand the how and why of measuring your progress. By measuring your accomplishments against your plan, you will see your progress. You will also learn to deal with your fear of the changes you will be making in your life.

Take pride in this journey of transformation. You will belong to a very select group of individuals who know how sweet success can be.

What's Your Take?

I want you to take some time and give some thought to how you will take action on what you have learned in this chapter. What you write down will help you get started on setting your goals. Remember to follow the five steps and to use all the tools you have put into your goal setting tool box.

Always look to raise the bar. Don't settle for the easy life. Live for a more rewarding life.

TAKE ACTION

Get Your Notebook

1. Write down one short-term goal that you wish to start with. Be sure to identify the facet and the time frame in which you feel you will be able to complete the goal.

2. Write the first action step that will move you toward the goal you indicated in the statement above.

3. Write an action step that will be a follow-up to the action step you wrote above.

4. Write down what accomplishing this goal will mean to you.

5. Write down the most important concept you learned from this chapter and how it impressed you.

STEP FIVE
Continued

Measuring Your Progress

CHAPTER 10

Measuring Your Progress

*Progress lies not in enhancing what is,
but in advancing toward what will be.*
Khalil Gibran

BEFORE YOU CAN MEASURE progress, you first must know the definition of what truly represents progress. Some will consider having written down a goal progress. Action steps achieved are not necessarily great accomplishments; however, they are measurable and important as to the direction you are heading. Action steps are not the ultimate goals, they are only the bits and pieces that, when achieved, will put you much closer to your ultimate goal.

Measuring the progress you have made is important. Every time you review an action step or goal, you should put the current results to the measure of progress. It should be clearly evident that you are moving toward your

> Stanislaw Jerzy Lec (1909–1966) was known for his aphorisms and poetry. He was hailed as one of Poland's great post-World War II writers. He challenged perceptions with his philosophical writings. He gave us this thought-provoking question:
>
> **"Is it not progress if a cannibal uses a fork?"**

goals. If it is not, then you must make some adjustments. Make the adjustment as soon as you see that something is moving you away from your goal.

Corrections and adjustments made early are smaller and easier. Wait too long and you will have to make drastic modifications. This will cost you valuable time and perhaps resources you cannot recover.

The best reason for utilizing a measurement is to record visually the progress made. If you are not reviewing weekly what progress you have made, you may find yourself not moving forward. You might even be only making motion and not movement.

Defining Progress

Progress can be defined as moving from one point to another point. In other words, moving forward from where you are now toward where you want to be. As long as the points are kept in as straight a line as possible, it is easy to see if you are moving toward your goal.

Your goal may be to get a driver's license. The first action step will be to go to the department of motor vehicles and pick up the most current copy of the driver's handbook or check online. Your second action step will be to read, study, and understand the information contained in the driver's handbook. The third action step is to pass the written test for your learner's permit. The next action step would be to practice driving until you are comfortable enough to take the driving test. Your next action step will be to schedule an appointment to take the driving test.

MEASURING YOUR PROGRESS

When you pass the test, you have completed your goal. Each action step is representative of the progress required to reach your goal. To complete any goal, you must go one step at a time.

Measuring Progress

I am old enough to remember, from back in elementary school, those charts with all the students' names. There were stars pasted in boxes showing the progress being made by reading the assigned books. In junior high there were charts used in wood shop to show completion of the various projects required to get a passing grade. These charts showed our progress, or lack thereof, for the whole world to see. Some of us were proud that we had stars or check marks indicating that we were on schedule to complete our goal. Some were embarrassed because they had not kept up with the work.

"Make measurable progress in reasonable time."

Jim Rohn

Progress needs to be measured. If it is not, accountability is unenforceable. Remember, these are your goals and your action steps that you choose to set. You are to hold yourself accountable for your progress toward your goal. You can make a chart and place stars or check marks where you have completed the required action steps. This will show the world that you are moving toward your goal. You certainly would not want to be embarrassed.

FIVE EASY STEPS TO ACHIEVING YOUR GOALS NOW!

CASE NOTE
The example in the paragraph above of getting a driver's license is a real case study showing how the goal and required action steps were planned and executed. We used this plan with individuals who needed to obtain their driver's license. Some would come back the next day to show me they had picked up the driver's handbook and stated they had begun reading it that night.

Some might take about three to four weeks to complete the action step. Others kept stating they would do it and after six months, it was evident they were not willing to make the effort to move forward. This was also reflected in how they motivated themselves to accomplish their other action steps and goals.

Over the years I have coached many individuals to change their vocational behaviors. Some were very willing and looked forward to our weekly review of how they were doing on their action steps and goals. Some would ask what else they could do to move forward faster. Others unfortunately would have a list of excuses for why they could not take action on the simple action steps they had set.

Excuses included having to watch their roommate's cat, being too busy, and not being able to find time to work on the action step. One decided to clean his room rather than complete the action step that would have moved him forward. Our weekly reviews measured the progress being made. Action steps were marked as completed for the majority, yet there were those who did not care or were just afraid to make a change in their life.

MEASURING YOUR PROGRESS

Measure progress and record it. This can be done on a chart or in a notebook. Where you keep the record and how you track it is not important. Measuring and recording is important.

As you do your weekly review, you might notice you are going a bit off course. Here is where you will need to make some adjustments. See if your action step was the correct one at this time. Was the action step not clearly defined? Were you missing some information needed to write it correctly? Is the action step dependent on someone else who failed to follow through?

You must account for not only accomplishing each action step or goal, but also account for the time it took. Nothing is wrong with completing an action step or goal ahead of the time you set for completion. The great benefit is that you can begin the next action step or goal sooner.

Please read aloud your final pledge in the box that follows. This will help you understand the meaning of taking action, and measuring your progress. Without taking action, you will never see progress. Measuring progress makes focusing on the important things clearer, sharper, and more achievable. Early discovery of areas of concern allows corrections to be made in a timely manner.

> **MY PLEDGE**
>
> *I will take action and measure all progress.*
> *I will record my progress and my achievements.*
> *I will enjoy this journey into a new paradigm.*

FIVE EASY STEPS TO ACHIEVING YOUR GOALS NOW!

Defeating Fear

When you see how much you have accomplished in a short period of time, you will be able to capitalize on your motivation. Your increased motivation will help you write better action steps and goals. This will give you more power to move toward your ultimate goals.

Fear is now displaced with increased confidence. You have turned on the light, and all the darkness has vanished. There is nothing left to fear. Be bold and take the chance. The odds are in your favor that you will achieve your goals as you let go of your fears.

This is why you need to measure progress and have it recorded. You need to visualize that you are truly making progress and it is measurable. It is great to see how far you have come from your beginning point and how much closer you are to your destination. The structure and habit of writing down your action steps and goals properly allows for the measuring and recording of their achievement. When you do the weekly review and see no progress, look at what you wrote down. If you did not keep your goals in accordance with the five steps, you will have to make adjustments or rewrite them so they can be achieved.

> *"Behold the turtle. He makes progress only when he sticks his neck out."*
>
> *James Bryant Conant*

If you don't measure your progress, how will you know if you have reached your goal? And if by accident you

MEASURING YOUR PROGRESS

happened to have achieved the goal, you might have missed a better opportunity, one that could have taken you faster and closer to your ultimate goal.

You will need to understand and recognize what is true and meaningful progress. Progress is that which has been accomplished leading toward your ultimate goal. Anything else is false progress and a drain on your energies and resources.

There are many ways to chart or record your progress. A three-ring binder, wall chart, or computer spreadsheet will suffice. The important thing to remember is to measure progress properly and then to record the progress. You will be the one who will be accountable for your progress or lack thereof. Don't blame others. You have the power and knowledge to make adjustments to keep you on track.

> *"One day's delay is another day's lack of progress."*
> Stuart Bowen

Always make sure you are progressing in a timely manner. Be accountable to the time frame you have committed to. When you fail to keep the time frame, you are only putting off your real progress. Keep a time line where you can always see it and try hard to stay on schedule.

Your goals and action steps should be given some priority. Just like on a "to do" list, you have to move the important items to the top. Don't think you have plenty of time. We only have so much, and then it's gone.

Be done with fear. You have planned this journey and should enjoy the experience. A little apprehension might be expected. Never let fear keep you from reaching and achieving your goals.

In the next chapter, you will learn about dealing with your new paradigms. Each action step and goal completed will begin a paradigm shift. You will learn how to deal with the increased knowledge, skills, and talents you will have obtained.

Reflect back on what you have learned so far. Employ these steps to move you to success.

What's Your Take?

I want you to take some time and give some thought to how you will measure your progress. What you write down can help you see different ways in which you can measure and record your progress.

Maintain your cadence of accountability. Stay focused and move steadily to your goals.

MEASURING YOUR PROGRESS

Get Your Notebook

1. Write down how you plan to measure the progress you are making on one of your goals.

2. Write how you will measure and record the progress made on your action steps.

3. Write how you plan to chart or record your accomplishments.

4. Write down how you will reward yourself for accomplishing your goals.

5. Write down the most important concept you learned from this chapter and how it impressed you.

STEP FIVE
Continued

New Paradigms

CHAPTER 11

The New Paradigms

*Everyone thinks of changing the world,
but no one thinks of changing himself.*
Leo Tolstoy

THIS CHAPTER IS ABOUT what you can expect as you complete your goals. This book was written to get you started on a lifelong journey of success, happiness, and contentment. As you finish one action step, you should immediately begin another. Attain one goal and create a new goal. Always be improving your life. Keep balance by working on all the facets of your life.

> Steve Prefontaine, a famous runner, once said:
>
> **"To give anything less than your best is to sacrifice the gift."**

You learned in chapter 1 the importance of keeping your goals simple, meaning not complicated, yet not necessarily easy. Chapter 2 dealt with keeping things realistic. It is nice to dream, but we must face reality, since that is the world in which we live. If a goal can't be reached then it is not achievable, as shown in chapter 3. Make sure to keep your action steps and goals achievable. Chapter 4 was about defining specifically what you want to achieve. This includes the proper time frame.

FIVE EASY STEPS TO ACHIEVING YOUR GOALS NOW!

And remember to keep your facets in balance depending on your stage in life, as shown in chapter 5. Balance is important—you must give the right priority to everything you do. Then when you have everything planned, you have to take action, as outlined in chapter 9. Only you can make this happen. You can do it.

Health

You deal with your health every day. Sometimes you don't give much thought to it, yet it is there with you at all times. When you get sick or get older, you tend to take more notice of your health. Knowledge of healthy eating habits, regular exercise, and visits to the doctor are necessary to remain at the top of your game.

"A man too busy to take care of his health is like a mechanic too busy to take care of his tools."

Spanish Proverb

There is physical health as well as mental health. Both need to be exercised to stay in proper working order. Play games requiring both physical and mental muscle. Read good books, play games requiring thought.

Remember, the health facet is the most important one. Without good health, the other facets suffer. You will not have the physical or mental energy to move forward.

As you work to accomplish your health goals, you will realize you have more energy, enthusiasm, and confidence. You will feel better about yourself. You will find your outlook on life improved. Being healthy is a good thing, and you deserve to have the best health.

Family

You are a member of a family. As such, you have certain obligations and responsibilities. A family can be defined as an immediate family unit or an organization you belong to. In a family you find comfort, support, and a sense of belonging to something greater than yourself. The power of family is what motivates you to take action, to do what must be done.

> *"A family is a unit comprised not only of children, but of men, women, an occasional animal, and the common cold."*
>
> Ogden Nash

You may have strained relationships with other family members. To gain peace you will have to reach out, forgive, and forget. You need this more than the family member you have the problem with. It will be good for your soul and your peace of mind.

Any goals you set that include the family will require you to have their input. Their involvement lets them take some ownership of your goal, and you will be surprised how much they will help you in achieving your goals.

When you achieve your goals to strengthen your family relationships, you will be creating a more loving environment. This is a place where all members of the family are willing to support your efforts. A sense of peace

Spirituality

Your spirituality begins with respecting what others believe, even if it is not in harmony with your own beliefs. How well you know your own religion is important. This might be one of those facets you do not put much stock into, but it will give you a center of balance greater than any other facet.

> *"A man is sane morally at thirty, rich mentally at forty, wise spiritually at fifty – or never!"*
>
> Dr. William Osler

Teach those you love what you believe. There are many faiths and religions in the world today. They all have one thing in common, and it is to do the most good for your fellow man. Rendering service on behalf of another is very rewarding. The reward cannot have a value placed on it. However, in your heart you know your service was well-received.

Your spirituality and your relationship with your maker is key to a happy life. At first you might not see things this way. But once you begin to humble yourself and accept the fact your success and growth are nothing more than blessings bestowed on you, then you will have more love and patience for others. Recognizing that possessions are just things, you will begin to see the rest of the world in a new light, one with hope for the future. Material possessions will not become as important as

> **CASE NOTE**
>
> Read, study, and discuss all the good books you can find. You will find them enlightening and uplifting. When things look darkest, you will find comfort in your beliefs. You are never alone if you have faith and conviction. Be active and participate. You will increase your respect for those you come to know.

they once seemed to be.

Self-Improvement/Education

Every day you must improve. Much of your early years were spent in formal education. Today this isn't enough. You must continually learn new things, procedures, and skills. If not, you will be left behind professionally.

> *"People seldom improve when they have no other model but themselves to copy after."*
>
> Oliver Goldsmith

Your mind also needs to exercise and be expanded through your hobbies and other interests. Try to learn something now you wished you would have learned years ago. There must be something you have always wanted to do and just never found the time. Set some time aside to learn those things now.

There are many conventions, trade shows, and craft shows all the time. You should make arrangements to attend one that offers you some knowledge, skill, or talent missing from your life. Leave fear behind and go boldly where you have always wanted to go. You will not regret learning something new.

Perhaps the greatest gift from self-improvement or education is having a greater understanding of life and the world around you. Sharing knowledge is a gift you can give. Knowledge has been described as power. Remember, with more knowledge comes more responsibility to use what you have and to continue to gain more.

Community

You are a part of the community. You do have an impact on what goes on. If you vote, you let your voice be heard. If you don't, then your silence won't be noticed. Be engaged in the good within your community. Seek those organizations that make a positive contribution to your community.

> **"When you are through changing, you are through."**
>
> Bruce Barton

There are so many good local organizations requiring your talents and skills. You can serve in the library helping to eliminate illiteracy. You may find your calling in spending time at the hospital reading, or just talking to a child or elderly individual. Don't feel that you cannot make a difference. You can be a hero to someone on any given day.

You will find many good organizations working with the local youth or elderly. Your community might have a civic theater where you can offer your assistance. Consider joining a veteran's organization if you are qualified to do so. They support local, state, and national programs to educate your community on how to be responsible citizens and to respect and honor the values that made this country what it is today.

Knowing what is happening in your community helps you become a better citizen. Supporting local organizations doing good works with your time and talents can be very rewarding. You will feel better when you know what you are doing has a very positive impact on the lives of your community family. Be sure to budget some time to share your knowledge, skills, and talents to improve your local, state, or national community. You will be proud of your service.

Career

You will spend a great deal of time working in a career or profession of your choice. The preparations you have made during your educational and training years will give you more choices from which to select. Whatever you decide to do for a living, make sure to do it well. Be the best at what you do. Stay on the top of your game by keeping up with the latest techniques and procedures. Don't let the competition get ahead of you.

> *"Choose a job you love, and you will never have to work a day in your life."*
> *Confucius*

FIVE EASY STEPS TO ACHIEVING YOUR GOALS NOW!

If you enjoy your work, you will awake each day with excitement and welcome anticipation of what the day will offer. If you truly enjoy what you do, it is no longer work. You will spend most of your waking hours in the pursuit of a career—make sure to pick one you can enjoy for many years.

Any vocation will give you challenges that require you to make decisions. There will be lots of stress and pressure placed on you to meet deadlines. Plan your day so you are in control. Having a pleasant work environment is essential to being happy. If you let work wear you down, you will take those frustrations home. Enjoy the hours you spend at work, and those you spend at home. Life is good. Make it so.

Finances

Financial knowledge is a must. This is something you have to deal with every day. Money worries cause problems that could have been avoided with some basic budget management. You don't have to have an advanced degree to handle money. Many millionaires do not have a college degree. They just learned how to make money work for them, rather than work for their money.

When you work for your money, you are a slave to it. It holds you back. It will not let you move forward. When you have your money work for you, it will give you a sense of freedom few have learned to appreciate.

Many look at success as being rich. Actually, success is being wealthy. These are two different mindsets. The rich try to show you what they have. The wealthy are far more secure and are not interested in showing off.

Be wise in how you use your money. Spend it wisely. Invest it intelligently. Care for it now, so it will care for you later.

> *"The only place success comes before work is in the dictionary."*
>
> *Vince Lombardi*

As you reach your financial goals, you will begin to understand that money is only a tool. If used properly, it can build a better future. If not, it will not provide what you expect from it and will be wasted. There are investment plans geared for whatever your risk tolerance might be. If you don't have the time or the inclination to manage your own finances, seek help from a professional financial expert.

You cannot succeed if you do not try. You can only achieve if you make the effort. You have to be willing to make some changes in your life. These are not painful changes, but changes for a better future.

Achieve your goals with passion and commitment. Never settle for less.

What's Your Take?

I want you to take some time and give some thought

FIVE EASY STEPS TO ACHIEVING YOUR GOALS NOW!

to what you have learned in this chapter. Keep it simple, realistic, achievable, well-defined, and take action so your goals can be achieved. You now have the seven facets so take action now. It is up to you to move forward.

Opportunities are everywhere. As you progress toward your goals, you will be amazed how many are waiting for you.

Get Your Notebook

1. Write down what you expect to accomplish having read this book.

2. Write down a time line for when you want to have met your most important goal.

3. Write a letter of appreciation to someone who will help or has helped you accomplish some of your goals.

4. Make a list of those you wish to share this new knowledge with so they will also change their lives for the better.

5. Write down the most important concept you learned from this chapter about the changes you hope to accomplish in the future.

STEP FIVE
Continued

Grab Your Tools

CHAPTER 12

Grab Your Tools and Get to Work

*Plans are only good intentions unless they
immediately degenerate into hard work.*
Peter Drucker

THIS CHAPTER IS the last in this book, but, there is much more to learn. As you begin to see changes in your life, you will see, hopefully, how much more your life has to offer. When you consider the opportunity you have to dream your dreams, set your own goals and reach them, you discover you belong to a very select group of individuals.

While there are no guarantees you will obtain every goal you set, you must at least try your best to reach them. This is your life, and you should plan it, live it, and enjoy it. Don't let obstacles hold you back. Be willing to make the changes in your life that give you what you desire. There are no short-cuts to accomplishing your goals.

> Gail Sheehy is an American author, lecturer, and journalist best known for her book *Passages*. She is credited with this quotation:
>
> **"If we don't change, we don't grow. If we don't grow, we aren't really living."**

You must work at them constantly in order to be successful. Change is what you want. To move from your current paradigm to a new and more fulfilling one is one of the most gratifying accomplishments you will ever make. Be bold and grow. Build on your past, don't just sit there.

Opportunity

You will find new opportunities waiting for you. But first you must become ready for them. Opportunity knocks on the door called "preparedness." If you are not prepared to recognize an opportunity or ready to act on it, you may have missed your chance. Life is not fair. It is worth it if you learn to see that life is about working smarter, not necessarily harder. Use your mind. Open your eyes and look for opportunities to achieve your goals.

"Opportunity is missed by most people because it is dressed in overalls and looks like work."

Thomas A. Edison

You have seen it; we all have. As we look back on our lives, we can see many opportunities we passed by without even a notice. We seem to be too focused on our immediate wants. We need to focus on the future in which we will live. An opportunity is what we make of it. Increased knowledge provides a chance that allows you to see the opportunities within your reach. Opportunities offer something very valuable and rare. If taken, they offer experience that challenges, builds, and tests us to see if we are ready to move forward.

Experience is what makes the difference in selecting the right candidate for a job, a promotion, or an appointment.

Learn to value your experiences as much as you do your possessions. Possessions can be taken from you; experience stays with you the rest of your life.

Responsibility

With change comes responsibility. When setting goals, you have a responsibility to make all possible efforts to accomplish them. It only takes a slight amount of extra effort to be a success. Some are content to just exist. Many have used excuses to explain away the lack of their motivation to move forward. No more excuses. Stand up and make your choice to be a better person. You are worth the effort.

> *"Anyone who can walk to the welfare office can walk to work."*
>
> Al Capp

We all have the same amount of time. How we use it sets us apart. Some will use it wisely, while others will waste it all away. Time is like money so be careful in how you spend it.

Ownership

Take ownership of your life. Take ownership of your goals. These are your goals. They will move you from where your are now, to where you want to be.

> *"Life is a journey that must be traveled no matter how bad the roads and accommodations."*
>
> Oliver Goldsmith

Have a positive attitude. Look for the positive things

FIVE EASY STEPS TO ACHIEVING YOUR GOALS NOW!

in life. Seek the positive in all you do. Don't be afraid to find ways to change your life. You have to live it, so you should live the life you want. Be grateful for all you have.

You should enjoy this journey of transformation. Owning your life makes you responsible for either the progress you make, or the lack thereof in achieving your goals. Look forward to the change. Take ownership and be proud of your accomplishments.

Limitations

Some of the limitations you will face are things you cannot control. If you cannot control it, you have to manage how you will deal with it. Keep a positive attitude and look for alternative ways of reaching your goals. There will sometimes be time constraints, and you will have to fit your life around them in order to achieve your goals. There are, however, many things that you can control—your attitude, your use of time, and which action step or goal you are pursuing.

> **"If you don't like something, change it. If you can't change it, change your attitude."**
>
> *Maya Angelou*

You also control your resources. Don't let them control you. You are in charge of this journey. You have to take the most efficient route, not just the easy route. What you learn and how you will use this new knowledge is the key to your accomplishments.

Stay focused on what you need to achieve. All else is a

distraction preventing you from moving forward. When you come to an obstruction or obstacle, take time to study your options. What you think is an obstruction can be, and most likely is, an opportunity for growth. No one promised this would be a cinch. Achieving your action steps and goals is hard work. But it is well worth it.

If you fail to use your resources you hurt your chances for success. The people who are your resources want you to achieve. They want to help you in your quest for a new you. The amount and quality of your resources are what makes the difference. Don't make the mistake of relying on just one resource. You have a time frame and you need to use your resource or resources to achieve your goals on schedule. Take charge and keep moving forward.

The Future

Your future is what you make it. The future is just a day away. There will be times when you will see rapid progress toward your goals. And there will be times when you feel nothing is moving at all. If you feel that you have stalled, work on another action step or goal. Don't waste time hoping for things to improve on their own.

> **"Always remember that the future comes one day at a time."**
> Dean Acheson

This is not a race. This is a steady progression of

planned actions resulting in you reaching your ultimate goals. This is about transforming you through small incremental changes in a particular direction. Progress is made one step at a time.

> **CASE NOTE**
>
> Over the years I have reached my goals when I have followed the principles in this book. Whenever I thought I was smarter than my plan, things did not go very well.
>
> When I stuck to my plan, did my due diligence, and held myself accountable for my progress, I was able to accomplish much more than I had planned.
>
> I know you will give each facet its own weight or value based on how you feel about the facet. I also know from observation and practice that keeping things balanced does make a difference.
>
> Just how successful you will be is up to you. Don't let life control you, learn to take control of it. I know you will succeed if you follow each of the five steps.

Your Tool Box

You have all the tools at your disposal now. It is up to you to take the action required to achieve your goals.

Use this book as a reference tool. Refer to it when you seem to be missing your mark. Tools are to be used, not just lugged around in a heavy box. Take care of your tools and they will take care of you.

GRAB YOUR TOOLS AND GET TO WORK

> *"The strong man meets his crisis with the most practical tools at hand. They may not be the best tools but they are available, which is all-important. He would rather use them, such as they are, than to do nothing."*
>
> Raymond Clapper

Reach out with your hands and grab the tools you need. Use each of them in the manner in which they were meant to be used. Find the proper tool to use and if it cannot be found in your tool box, go out and get it. Remember, no excuses.

Ask yourself if you are now ready for the challenge. If you are, then get going. Don't let life pass you by. Do all you can to move yourself to where you want to be. Don't let others hold you back. See obstacles as a possible opportunity for growth. Enjoy this journey. There is no looking back. Always move forward toward your goals. You will be glad you did.

Enjoy this journey and the changes you make. You deserve the best. Now is your opportunity so take hold of it.

Do yourself proud! Make success part of your daily routine.

Hold yourself to a higher standard and you will see a more successful you.

FIVE EASY STEPS TO ACHIEVING YOUR GOALS NOW!

Good luck.

Thank you for reading this book.

Appendixes

Personal Inventory Summary

THIS SUMMARY FORM will help you evaluate where you are now (your starting point) and where you would like to be (your destination). This form is your ready reference where you begin to set your goals. Since you will be doing your own evaluation, you will have to be totally honest. Your assessment should be on the conservative side.

You may feel you are better than you really are. This is the time to be a bit humble. Begin with a few goals that you will be able to achieve quickly. Once you understand how this works, you will be able to set more detailed goals. Once you complete this personal inventory summary, you can transfer some of the information on the facet worksheets as action steps and goals. You are the builder of your future. You now have all the tools you need. Good luck and enjoy the journey.

Note: Your evaluation is based on a scale of one to four. One indicates a serious need for change. Two indicates a need for change. Three indicates a need for some minor changes. Four indicates that there is room for change. Most of your evaluation numbers will be one, two, or three. Even though we think we are a four, there is always some room for positive changes in our habits and behaviors.

The statements or questions are meant to get you thinking about what you should be working on. Check the evaluation number where you feel you are currently. Then, write out your goals and some action steps that will be required to accomplish those goals. When you are done you can transfer the goal and action steps to the worksheets.

FIVE EASY STEPS TO ACHIEVING YOUR GOALS NOW!

Health Facet

Based on your height, how much should you weigh? Do you need to set a goal to reach your desired weight?

☐ 1 ☐ 2 ☐ 3 ☐ 4

Goal and Action Step Ideas:

_____
_____
_____
_____
_____

Are you in need of a physical exam? When was the last time you had lab tests done?

☐ 1 ☐ 2 ☐ 3 ☐ 4

Goal and Action Step Ideas:

_____
_____
_____
_____
_____

PERSONAL INVENTORY SUMMARY

Do you remember the last time you went to the dentist, or had your teeth cleaned?

☐ 1   ☐ 2   ☐ 3   ☐ 4

Goal and Action Step Ideas:

_____
_____
_____
_____
_____

When was the last time you had your eyes examined or had a new prescription for corrective lenses?

☐ 1   ☐ 2   ☐ 3   ☐ 4

Goal and Action Step Ideas:

_____
_____
_____
_____
_____

FIVE EASY STEPS TO ACHIEVING YOUR GOALS NOW!

Do you need to change your eating habits to include a healthier diet?

☐ 1　　☐ 2　　☐ 3　　☐ 4

Goal and Action Step Ideas:

_____

_____

_____

_____

_____

Do you have a regular exercise program for both your body and brain?

☐ 1　　☐ 2　　☐ 3　　☐ 4

Goal and Action Step Ideas:

_____

_____

_____

_____

_____

PERSONAL INVENTORY SUMMARY

Family Facet

Do you need to work on your relationships with your immediate family members?

☐ 1   ☐ 2   ☐ 3   ☐ 4

Goal and Action Step Ideas:

_____
_____
_____
_____
_____

How is your relationship with your extended family? Your social family?

☐ 1   ☐ 2   ☐ 3   ☐ 4

Goal and Action Step Ideas:

_____
_____
_____
_____
_____

FIVE EASY STEPS TO ACHIEVING YOUR GOALS NOW!

How are your relationships with your neighborhood family?
How are your relationships with your church family?

☐ 1   ☐ 2   ☐ 3   ☐ 4

Goal and Action Step Ideas:

_____
_____
_____
_____

How are your current relationships with your old friends, classmates, military buddies, etc.?

☐ 1   ☐ 2   ☐ 3   ☐ 4

Goal and Action Step Ideas:

_____
_____
_____
_____

PERSONAL INVENTORY SUMMARY

Spirituality Facet

How is your relationship with your Heavenly Father? With his Son, Jesus Christ? Or your own God?

☐ 1 ☐ 2 ☐ 3 ☐ 4

Goal and Action Step Ideas:

_____

_____

_____

_____

_____

Do you feel you are giving honest service to others?

☐ 1 ☐ 2 ☐ 3 ☐ 4

Goal and Action Step Ideas:

_____

_____

_____

_____

_____

FIVE EASY STEPS TO ACHIEVING YOUR GOALS NOW!

How well do you know your own religion?

☐ 1 ☐ 2 ☐ 3 ☐ 4

Goal and Action Step Ideas:

_____
_____
_____
_____
_____

How is your relationship with members of your church congregation?

☐ 1 ☐ 2 ☐ 3 ☐ 4

Goal and Action Step Ideas:

_____
_____
_____
_____
_____

PERSONAL INVENTORY SUMMARY

Are you currently attending your church regularly? Are you participating in the social activities your church provides?

☐ 1   ☐ 2   ☐ 3   ☐ 4

Goal and Action Step Ideas:

_____
_____
_____
_____

Are you paying a full tithe and contributing to assist the needy?

☐ 1   ☐ 2   ☐ 3   ☐ 4

Goal and Action Step Ideas:

_____
_____
_____
_____

FIVE EASY STEPS TO ACHIEVING YOUR GOALS NOW!

Self-Improvement/Education Facet

Do you feel a need to increase your educational level to get a better job?

☐ 1   ☐ 2   ☐ 3   ☐ 4

Goal and Action Step Ideas:

_____
_____
_____
_____
_____

Are there some technical or certificate training programs you need to complete to get a better job?

☐ 1   ☐ 2   ☐ 3   ☐ 4

Goal and Action Step Ideas:

_____
_____
_____
_____
_____

PERSONAL INVENTORY SUMMARY

Can you list any skills or experiences you need to get a job or a promotion where you currently work?

☐ 1   ☐ 2   ☐ 3   ☐ 4

Goal and Action Step Ideas:

_____

_____

_____

_____

_____

Do you have any hobbies or special interests that you would like to have more knowledge or skills in?

☐ 1   ☐ 2   ☐ 3   ☐ 4

Goal and Action Step Ideas:

_____

_____

_____

_____

_____

FIVE EASY STEPS TO ACHIEVING YOUR GOALS NOW!

Do you have some talents or skills you would like to improve?

☐ 1   ☐ 2   ☐ 3   ☐ 4

Goal and Action Step Ideas:

_____
_____
_____
_____
_____

Are there any crafts you would like to learn how to do or share with others?

☐ 1   ☐ 2   ☐ 3   ☐ 4

Goal and Action Step Ideas:

_____
_____
_____
_____
_____

PERSONAL INVENTORY SUMMARY

Would you like to travel to see new places? Would you like to learn a second or additional language?

☐ 1 ☐ 2 ☐ 3 ☐ 4

Goal and Action Step Ideas:

_____
_____
_____
_____
_____

Do you have any skills, talents, or special knowledge that you can share with another individual?

☐ 1 ☐ 2 ☐ 3 ☐ 4

Goal and Action Step Ideas:

_____
_____
_____
_____
_____

FIVE EASY STEPS TO ACHIEVING YOUR GOALS NOW!

Do you need to improve your computer skills?

☐ 1   ☐ 2   ☐ 3   ☐ 4

Goal and Action Step Ideas:

_____

_____

_____

_____

Would you like to improve your public speaking ability?

☐ 1   ☐ 2   ☐ 3   ☐ 4

Goal and Action Step Ideas:

_____

_____

_____

_____

PERSONAL INVENTORY SUMMARY

Community Facet

How well do you know the issues within your community, county, state, or nation?

☐ 1 ☐ 2 ☐ 3 ☐ 4

Goal and Action Step Ideas:

_____
_____
_____
_____
_____

Do you read the voters' pamphlet before voting to understand the issues and the candidates? Do you go vote?

☐ 1 ☐ 2 ☐ 3 ☐ 4

Goal and Action Step Ideas:

_____
_____
_____
_____
_____

FIVE EASY STEPS TO ACHIEVING YOUR GOALS NOW!

How much time do you volunteer to help your community, civic organizations, youth groups, or senior citizens?

☐ 1   ☐ 2   ☐ 3   ☐ 4

Goal and Action Step Ideas:

_____
_____
_____
_____
_____

How well do you know the history of your community, county, state, or nation?

☐ 1   ☐ 2   ☐ 3   ☐ 4

Goal and Action Step Ideas:

_____
_____
_____
_____
_____

PERSONAL INVENTORY SUMMARY

Career Facet

Are you currently in the career you really want? Are you willing to stay there and seek promotions?

☐ 1   ☐ 2   ☐ 3   ☐ 4

Goal and Action Step Ideas:

_____
_____
_____
_____
_____

What skills, talents, or knowledge do you need to get a promotion at work or to get the job you really want?

☐ 1   ☐ 2   ☐ 3   ☐ 4

Goal and Action Step Ideas:

_____
_____
_____
_____
_____

FIVE EASY STEPS TO ACHIEVING YOUR GOALS NOW!

What can you do to enlarge your position to merit more pay and responsibility?

☐ 1   ☐ 2   ☐ 3   ☐ 4

Goal and Action Step Ideas:

_____
_____
_____
_____
_____

Do you feel safe in your current job? Are you vulnerable to an economic down turn or downsizing? Do you have options?

☐ 1   ☐ 2   ☐ 3   ☐ 4

Goal and Action Step Ideas:

_____
_____
_____
_____
_____

PERSONAL INVENTORY SUMMARY

Finances Facet

Do you have enough money to support yourself and your family?

☐ 1   ☐ 2   ☐ 3   ☐ 4

Goal and Action Step Ideas:

_____
_____
_____
_____
_____

Are you saving for a house or a new vehicle? Do you have enough in savings or other assets?

☐ 1   ☐ 2   ☐ 3   ☐ 4

Goal and Action Step Ideas:

_____
_____
_____
_____
_____

FIVE EASY STEPS TO ACHIEVING YOUR GOALS NOW!

Are you setting aside enough for your self-improvement or education and for your children?

☐ 1   ☐ 2   ☐ 3   ☐ 4

Goal and Action Step Ideas:

_____

_____

_____

_____

_____

Do you currently use a budget and stick to it? If not, do you really know where your money is going?

☐ 1   ☐ 2   ☐ 3   ☐ 4

Goal and Action Step Ideas:

_____

_____

_____

_____

_____

PERSONAL INVENTORY SUMMARY

Are you saving and investing for your retirement? Do you have a retirement plan?

☐ 1 ☐ 2 ☐ 3 ☐ 4

Goal and Action Step Ideas:

_____

_____

_____

_____

_____

Are you working on leaving a legacy to your heirs, your favorite organization, or a worthy cause?

☐ 1 ☐ 2 ☐ 3 ☐ 4

Goal and Action Step Ideas:

_____

_____

_____

_____

_____

FIVE EASY STEPS TO ACHIEVING YOUR GOALS NOW!

Additional areas you wish to set goals in:

A. _____

_____

☐ 1   ☐ 2   ☐ 3   ☐ 4

Goal and Action Step Ideas:

_____
_____
_____
_____
_____

B. _____

_____

☐ 1   ☐ 2   ☐ 3   ☐ 4

Goal and Action Step Ideas:

_____
_____
_____
_____
_____

SIMPLE BUDGET

Month		Year	
Income		Projected	Actual
Salary/Wages			
Passive Income			
Other Income			
	Totals		
Expenses		Projected	Actual
Rent/Mortgage/Housing			
Food			
Transportation/Auto			
Insurance			
Clothing			
Utilities			
Phone/Internet			
Medical			
Savings			
Investments			
Rainy Day Fund			
Charitable Contributions			
Education			
Loans			
Other			
	Totals		
	Income		
	- Expenses		
	Over/(Short)		

GOAL SHEET

My Goal	
Facet	
Start Date	Target Date
My Objective	
My Plan	
My Resources	
My Results	

ACTION STEP SHEET

Action Step No. _____ For My Goal:
Facet
Start Date   Target Date
My Objective
My Plan
My Resources
My Results

www.ingramcontent.com/pod-product-compliance
Lightning Source LLC
Chambersburg PA
CBHW061303110426
42742CB00012BA/2035